THE WAY OF THE LOVER

THE WAY OF THE LOVER

The Awakening & Embodiment
Of The Full Human

Robert Augustus Masters

XANTHYROS FOUNDATION

Copyright © 1988 by Robert Augustus Masters
Published by XANTHYROS FOUNDATION

First Printing April 1989
Second Printing November 1989

Printed and bound in Canada

ISBN: 0-88925-922-4 paperback

Take me to the bottom of your pain
Take me to the weave of your true name
Take me, take me deep, take me steep
Let's stretch to make the leap
Let's go to where love must also weep
Take me, take me over the rise,
Take me past all your goodbyes
Let's shine through our every disguise
Let's go to where insights lose their mind
Let's go to where love is never blind
Take me, take me in, take me through your hidden door
Take me, take me in, take me right to your core
Let's throw away our every alibi
Let's go to where love cannot lie

Contents

PART III: SONGS & INCANTATIONS

PART IV: WELCOMING THE PREPARATORY FIRE

Prelude

The Way Of The Lover is not about fulfilling ourselves within our dreams, nor about finding a more consoling dream, but rather is about the art of recognizing and awakening from *all* our dreams, without any dissociation or recoil from passion, desire, attachment, intimacy, or any other facet of a fully human life. Through making room for all that we are, not metaphysically, but *literally*, level upon level, we contact and *embody* a very different kind of fulfillment, not one that just pleasurably sedates us, emptying us of the tension of unilluminated desire, but one that rejuvenates and alerts us, re-establishing us in full-bodied, radiant communion with the Truth of what we fundamentally are — thus do we become our own fulfillment, simultaneously individuated and surrendered to the Source of All, saddling nothing with the obligation to make us feel better, freeing ourselves from self-constriction and its compensatory addictions, ever rising from the totality of ourselves, breathing more and more integrity into our stride, letting ourselves be a meeting-place of grief and joy, a potent and throbbingly human intersection of both the mortal and the Everlasting.

The Way Of The Lover reveals not a step-by-step path or system, paved with doctrine, idealism, and compulsive ritual, but an ever-new passage, not from here to there, but from here to a *deeper* here — it is not a bridge over Life's troubles, but a gutsy, luminous entry right into *and* through the very heart of them, a journey that honours no morality except that generated by the awakening process.

The Way Of The Lover is not the way of the introvert (seeking consolation and immunity through the exploitation of inwardness), the extrovert (seeking these through obsessive outwardness), or the convert (seeking these through cultic membership), nor is it the way of childishness (devotionalism and neurotic dependence), adolescence (deified or self-glamourizing independence), romanticism (false oneness), or liberalism (false tolerance), nor is it the way of any other egocentric strategy — its structuring is not preordained, nor confined to already-penned instruction and dogma, but arises naturally and spontaneously in exquisitely empathetic correspondence to one's current needs and circumstances.

The lover is a psychospiritual outlaw, free of all cultural taboos, yet profoundly responsible. In the lover, dependence and independence are not in opposition, nor in parasitic collusion, but rather in juicy embrace, potently unleashing through their sensitive yet dynamic interplay a fecund, heartfelt resonance with the obviousness of Eternal interdependence and interrelatedness. Again and again, the Ecstasy, Suffering, and seamless Wonder of Existence are uninhibitedly embodied by the lover. The lover stays wounded, innocently yet knowingly raw, avoiding the lure of indifference and "spiritual" detachment, inhabiting an intimacy both intensely personal and transcendent, clearly demonstrating that awareness and feeling need not be separated.

The lover is not an ideal, nor a fantasy, but only the full humanness of us. Neither nice nor mean, neither sentimental nor cynical, neither hopeful nor despairing, the lover is only present, excruciatingly and deliciously alive, with eyes both stormy and calm, and flesh shining with spirit-force, unburdened by reasonableness, ever flirting with the edge of the Edge, flowing with both leap and stance, lustily outdancing every surrogate self, knots dissolving in sacred thrill — the lover is not on a mission, nor is driven by spiritual ambition, nor is looking for permission, but is a conscious prism for the Source, a midwife, an orgasmic medium, a wilderness, a magical softness, an ecstatic ground-edness, a fire, a force, a subtle delicacy, a bud with newborn lips moistly aquiver, a forest giant piercing the sky, a sinewy exultation and voluptuous flowering nectared and all aswoon, overflowing with the hello in grief, the vulnerability in anger, the silence in passion, and the joy of each new leaf, richly veined with the humour of Christ, the lust of Buddha, the labour of Lao Tzu, the non-effort of Gurdjieff, the virginal ordinariness of the Avatar and the brilliance of every truly human star and the pure cry of the deepest human longing, the rainbowed shout of the unfurling heart, the radiantly fluid power of true center, the dying into Undying Life, the necessary heartbreak speechless with fearlessly upstart green...

The lover is pristine need, mind-free need, lucid and magnificently personified need, ravishingly naked, streaming with natural integrity.

For the lover, ecstasy is not the goal, but the foundation — the lover knows that ecstasy cannot be produced, but only expressed and shared.

The lover neither exploits his or her vitality, nor flees it for subtler rewards, as is all too common in meditative practice, but only embodies it from toe to crown, thus spanning both West and East, again and again losing balance only to find a deeper balancing, unambivalently standing his or her true ground, without making spiritual real estate out of it. Paradox is not a problem for the lover, but the very matrix of Being, the primordial and unavoidable anatomical design of manifest existence.

The lover is not within, nor without, but simply here, living *as* the very core of each moment, existing in essence as a quality, a condition, a choice, that cries out for complete incarnation. As such, the lover is but a potentiality awaiting animation, a fluxing latticework of encoded desire asking to be fleshed out and fully lived.

This book is about the awakening of the lover, the natural human, the passionate witness, the full-blooded wholeness of ourselves, and it is also about the turning away from this; it does not distance itself from its subject matter with irony and understatement, but plunges in, intimate with both its forcefulness and its subtlety, letting both scientist and poet speak with one tongue, letting both the shout and the whisper uncover the way of the lover.

It is not for agreement or disagreement that this book asks, but for awakened feeling. Let it stir you, shake you, cry with you, enrage and uncage you, jolt you, loosen you; let it undress you, let it mess and caress you, let it spelunk you, debunk you, unmonk and undrunk you, let it unclench your hidden grip, let it touch you; and let it sing to you, let it wing and sting you, let it curse with you, let it dance you true, let it take you high and take you low, let it take you to the bottom of your pain, let it take you to the weave of your true name, let it take you to where love cannot lie, let it flame through your every alibi ...

Speak with this book. Read it aloud with one or more intimates. Enrich your reading with periodic eyes-shut listenings to the tapes listed at the back of the book, all of which are spontaneous talks delivered from the same place as this book was written. Meet me through the pages, and greet me where joy and pain disappear into sun and rain, where hearts must break, where the fire is both heat and light, where outside and inside are lovers, where we can only be the Truth we must speak.

The Way Of The Lover was mine to write, and is mine to give, but is ours to live.

Ride it all the way.

Use me.

Robert Augustus Masters
West Vancouver, December 24, 1988

Part I

**Breathing Integrity
Into
Our Stride**

1

The Inside And Outside
Of Self-Fragmentation

Almost all of us are without a true center of being — we literally have gone to pieces, fleeing deep integration, repairing our fracturing of self only peripherally, rarely doing anything more than just getting by as a self-enclosed, uneasily governed crowd of fragments. Each fragment, when given sufficient attention, tends to automatically refer to itself as "I." However, all these "I's" are not really selves, or discrete entities, but rather are only habits, or activities of utter mechanicalness.

Our dominant "I" is but the fragment granted the most attention. It is a puppet, a mannequin obsessed with its own continuation, a personalized parody of a real human, viewing everything as either verification or condemnation of its assumed identity. It is terrified of Death. It is addicted to distracting itself from whatever might expose its charade. Again and again, it impales itself on its altar of predictability, consolation, and anaesthetizing familiarity, even as it desperately seeks novelty, not to mention relief from the pain of being itself...

When just about all of us say "I," we are only unknowingly identifying with our dominant fragment of being, embodying its imperatives, speaking its mind and raising its flag, letting it shape our life, arrange our face, cripple our stride, and ossify our misguided pride. We further reinforce our case of mistaken identity by associating with other like-minded "individuals," forming cultic groups or organizations, ranging from the very small (a couple) to the very large (a religion).

Our overseeing fragment of being is usually a begrudging coalition between two very different fragments, one of which is much more visible, or apparently active, than the other. The tension, or opposition, between them both binds and sustains them — they cannot exist without each other, no matter how strongly they malign or sabotage one another, no matter how vehemently they deny each other existence. Instead of recognizing their perverse union, they project each other out onto their environment, staying in contact through a paranoid surveillance of one another. They seek power over, not power with. They do not love, but only bounce between sentimentality and cynicism. They crave wholeness, but seek for it through a dissolving of their boundaries (preferably when as intoxicated, stimulated, or romantically deluded as possible), rather than through an expansion of them. They are but dreamers dreaming they are awake, simultaneously hating and clinging to their marriage to each other, ever seeding their offspring with their insanity...

Beneath this governing polarity seethe and squirm many other pretenders to the throne of self. They resent being parented by such an obvious incompetent, loudly and earnestly proclaiming, when given center stage by the right set of conditions, that they could govern far more wisely and humanely. When given such an opportunity, however, they do no better than their usual overseer, for they too are but a personified fragment, a fake self, a posturing of potential energy committed to an utterly predictable script. What the fragments do not know (for they cannot stand apart from what they are, so as to be able to authentically witness themselves) is that they cannot escape from each other — they, be they lewd or prude, revolutionary or stationary, right-wing or left-wing, humble or greedy, are all in it together, all of them parts of a forgotten or repressed unity, all of them expressions, however twisted, of something that both includes *and* transcends them.

And is it not obvious that the above applies not only to the so-called individual, but also to human culture itself? Does not our society, in its mind-made moralities, its unillumined dramatics, its rigid structuring, its obsession with entertainment, its taboo against awakening, its compulsive compartmentalization, accurately reflect and magnify the fragmentation and suppression of being that plagues almost all of us? And is not government but a massive version of ego (ego being the headquarters of our fragmentation of self)?

As long as unconscious fragmentation persists, there will be war and all sorts of lesser violences (including that of forced peace). No form of government, however benign or humane, can prevent this, for the very same reason that one's dominant fragment of being cannot bring about inner peace — its very existence as a governing force depends on the suppression of the rest of one. Government, like ego, cannot *truly* serve all that it oversees, simply because its *peripheral* positioning leaves it ignorant of what is central, or essential to all. Its police and military forces are equivalent to the blind judgmentalness and aberrated conscience of ego. Subjugation is demanded and rewarded. Robotic conformity is thoroughly inculcated; non-conformist leanings are channeled into preprogrammed outlets, or are given a little more room if they are profitably entertaining, but not so offensive as to be unabsorbable by the mainstream of society. Bureaucracy replaces trust. Guilt fills churches and empties hearts. Love is reduced to an ideal, and a lesser love breeds itself silly...

No form of government truly works. No form of religion works. Nor does any therapeutic strategy, however sophisticated, work. Why not? Simply because they, like ego, addictively seek submission to their structure or ideology. They are only a form of collective ego, bound up in their misguided morality.

So what does work? Whatever arises from a heartfelt *and* conscious embodiment of that which both includes *and* transcends all fragmentation, both individual and cultural. Whatever stems from awakening, not a dissociative, strategically detached awakening, but rather a full-blooded awakening that requires no withdrawal whatsoever from passion, grief, anger, lust, love, and ecstasy. Whatever is done from a foundation rooted in mind-free identification with the totality of oneself...

Only those with a stably established center of being can do good. When others "do" good, it is accidental, little more than a positive byproduct of their conditioning, rather than a conscious act — one moment, they are helping someone in need, and the next moment, they're participating in something that only contributes to the ill-health of the Earth. Those who are asleep to their true nature cannot be trusted, for they are strangers to integrity, held together not by center, but by enslavement to a morality imposed from without; even if they possess what appears to be integrity, it is not "theirs," and therefore could, if confronted by the right circumstances, easily mutate into something very different.

A society that truly works has not, as far as I know, existed, except in imagination and nostalgia, because such a society would have to be made up of awakened individuals (or those in whom center does not come and go with shifts in mood or circumstance) committed to living together, not as monks or renunciates or any other kind of escapist, but as *full* humans, turned away from none of what they are. The effort required to establish even the base of this is work that very, very few are willing to endure, and those few are not always necessarily inclined toward forming community. Tremendous courage, stamina, humour, and intelligence are required. Spiritual ambition and enthusiasm are of no use. The transition from romance to love, from machine to human, from egocentricity to essence-centricity, must be made if real community is to be...

Without true center, that which is suppressed (in self or in community) will sabotage the rest, sooner or later. With center, that which is suppressed can be safely externalized and made good use of — even the most extreme violence, when fully and sanely exposed, can be well used, for when it is illuminated and breathed loose by the forces of center, it becomes but available Life-energy, raw vitality in the *service* of one's being. However, violence cannot be safely released and transformed by those who have no center; in fact, release in such a case only manifests as cruelty, distress, sadism, mind-fucking, and war. Those without center refer to the repression of such forces or activities as peace, not seeing that their repression is but a kind of socially acceptable violence.

The uneasy truce that characterizes both the so-called individual and human culture does no one any good. Ending it does not necessarily mean chaos, ruin, and war, nor does it mean another kind of truce or government, nor does it mean peace. Ending it, really ending it, is not possible without awakening, and until that process is *active* in one, there is no point in trying to see what's going to happen, or in getting worried about what might happen. Awakening, or the end of self-fragmentation, creates its own morality, its own imperatives. To say what these are is of no use to one who has not made their own awakening top priority. Don't look ahead. Look at who's doing the looking. Look *inside* your looking. Look and leap at the same time, knowing that it's always time for the sacred reunion of all that you are...

2

The Teacher Is Everywhere

The teacher is everywhere.

There is no need to personify the giver or givers of a particular lesson. They are but the mediums for what we most deeply require, shaped by our current condition. That is, if we notice them at all. With misguided ease, we all too readily deny the presence of our testing, and go searching for a tutor or guru who fits not our need to awaken, but rather our craving to be pampered, inflated, and reassuringly distracted within our self-entrapment.

Nevertheless, the teacher does not take our turning away personally. The teacher both exists apart from us, and is created by us. Do you not see this? How we mutilate form to suit our view? How we enthusiastically lean toward the new, but only reinforce the obsolete us? How we scream and scheme for more, but won't open the door? How we proclaim love, and fuck away our desire? How we want to be loved before we will love? How we so sincerely lie about our lies, and keep painting holy wings on our disguise?

The teacher is everywhere.

The drama of teacher and pupil is enacted for our benefit. We are the stage for it, as well as the audience, and yet still beggars for our own applause. Is it of any use for me to say this? Have you already misunderstood it? Would you rather be right than true? Would you rather crumple this page up, like you have crumpled yourself, leaving yourself in an air-conditioned wastebasket, unread, unfelt, joining so many others in spiritual suicide? Or have you lost interest in finding yet another consoling logic for your exile? Or are you still chained to the courtroom, swollen by the intrigue of your trial, ever defending your denial?

The teacher is available, now. And the teacher is not even a teacher, but only a relationship, an interdependence, awaiting you so that it might come fully alive. So that it might burn bright and all around, its flames consuming your every name, until you stand up sane, no longer addicted to crouching behind blame.

Give yourself permission to die. Give yourself velvet thunder, rolling through your hidden sky, revealing a solitary temple whose pillars are throbbing lightning, and whose floor is moaning earth, all aflower, all aburst with rainbow greens sweetly aquiver, streaming with nectared song and butterflies with wings of iridescent ivory and lace, all of it dancing so fluid and so deep, ever spinning out a sacred circle. O Give yourself the space to leap. Take the jump, and keep taking it. Keep breaking your own rules. Keep giving a belly to your flights, and a heart to your murderous impulse, and a welcome to your darkest nights.

Give yourself permission to die, to cry, to fly, to pump holy passion into your every goodbye. Make sky. Soar through valleys of heartbreaking green and over peaks of virgin white, drinking in every tiny scene, every grassblade's thrusting toward the light, every farmer's squint, every taxi driver's shout, every bloody step through the cannon-castled snowfields, every junkie's oblivion, every unheard cry, every break-through, every breakdown, every butchering, every kindness, every-one's everything, all of it shrieking and groaning and laughing and hating and rising and falling and birthing and puking and singing through and through, winging through the prism, the prism of you, of you, of you... This is your myth. This is your exploding canal, your recurring tunnel, your wall, your adventure, your dream. It is far more real than you.

Become real.

Embody Truth. Shine true, shine through every view, shine steady, shine deep, shine pure, outshine every you...

The teacher only brings us to this, to the undying intensity and ease of utterly unreasonable bliss. Ecstasy is not escape, but love, the celebration of undiluted love, the shout of the awakened heart. Ecstasy does not avoid pain, but nor does it settle for the scenarios painted by pain and signed by mind. Ecstasy is not the goal of human existence, but the very foundation, simultaneously solid and transparent.

And ecstasy is more you than the you reading this. Too much of the time, you are but a jostling, argumentative, loveless mob of habits that insists on referring to itself as a somebody, namely you. And you are the witness of this. And you are the source of all witnessing. And you are the forgetting of all this, the terrible knot pulled tight between sternum and spine. And you are my lover, forever, our flesh of mud and stars, our flesh married to time, even as it moves to an eternal rhyme, beyond all notions of glory and crime.

Do you not remember me? Do you not know me? Do you not feel the one who now writes this? Do you not recognize the pulsating current, the unshackled aliveness that leaps from this page, the suddenly familiar demand, the invitation that will not go away, no matter what you do or say?

The fingers that type this only seem to belong to me. They serve a will that is both mine and thine. And do not your fingers now slowly run up my spine, joining me in every line, until our insights cannot help but lose their mind? Does not your heart encircle mine, and mine yours? And in this, is there any need to create the theatre of a teacher? Is not the teacher everywhere, lucidly present, juicily available, when we stop peering through the warped frames of our dreams?

So let us come together, and enjoy every kind of weather, every bit of common ground, every distinction, without needing any nirvanic extinction. This is God.

3

The Impulse To Awaken

The impulse to awaken is not evident in most people, and even when it is, it tends to get very little conscious attention. Other things seem more important. Details, information, and persona-conservation clutter and obscure the essential. There *seems* to be so, so much to do.

We all too easily arrange everything, rehearsing ourselves to death, automatically assuming that we are awake. Our snore, however well-intentioned or ecologically-minded, only chainsaws the wilderness, leaving us in a wasteland strewn with the ruins of ourselves, governed by personifications of our compensatory reactions, while a broken child sobbingly writhes within us, its cries all but lost in the bustling static of our slumber...

True awakening gradually undoes this madness, unveiling Truth's horizons, greening the moment, levelling the monuments of unillumined ambition, sensitizing us to far, far more than our habits' mission. Such awakening is coincident with ecstasy; neither produces the other. Both arise naturally and spontaneously when the impulse to awaken is given heartfelt attention, not just in the midst of meditative absorption or primal breakthrough, but in the midst of whatever is happening.

All our longings, however gross or sweet or twisted or subtle, are but reflections of our longing to awaken, to enter and live and give the fullness of what we truly are.

So let us go into the primordial core of all our longings, and let us go with luminous passion, welcoming whatever we must pass through, making as much room for our hurt, lust, and violence as for our joy and compassion, letting our native wildness of being dive deep, climb steep, sing, weep, and leap, and fly, fly across open ground, fly, fly through every sky, its very movement its illumination...

That is, let us work with what is occurring right now, not with its secondary ramifications, but with its primary *obviousness* — if, for example, you are caught in a self-imposed vise-grip around your chest (as in emotional contraction), and it keeps giving you a headache, don't bother taking aspirin, getting a neck massage, or trying to therapize or meditate away your headpain, but instead simply notice the vise-grip you are in, and notice the fact that *you* are doing it even as you *feel* it directly, not in terms of its branchings and side-effects, but as the very clenching that it at essence is. Do this, and a loosening will gradually occur, *not* as a counter-effort to self-contraction, but as a result of *ceasing* to give energy to such contractedness.

Awakening is not a byproduct of hope, meditative strategy, guru-worship, "enlightenment" seminars, or loyalty to a particular doctrine or belief system. In fact, those who would indulge in such activities are but escapists and integrity-rapists, looking for no more than immunity, enslaving themselves to their method, reducing even meditation to no more than a remedy — they have but fled the feeling dimension of their being, finding refuge in caves or high-rises of mind, especially those that are mystically or metaphysically furnished.

Awakening is a fire, a living brilliance; what we are up to in this moment is its fuel. Once the process of awakening has begun, it must be tended with great care — it may sprout up easily, but to really take firm root, it must receive a continuity of care. It is of little use to just get enthusiastic about awakening when the mood hits you; doing so actually weakens the awakening impulse.

So what can be done when we are not only not in the mood, but are in the throes of some incredibly contracted state? The key is not to just detach ourselves and play witness, but rather to *consciously feel* our way right to the heart of our self-suppression. This, done consistently, is the embodiment of the passionate witness...

No recoil. This is not about feeling better, nor about trying to feel better, but about getting to the heart of the matter. If feeling better is the goal, then we only lose ourselves in our strategies to alter our condition. It is crucial to stop detaching and dissociating from our pain. What is wrong with attachment? Why flee it? Why make an adversary out of it? It is utterly natural. One who is awakening does not make a problem out of attachment, nor out of anything else; their letting go is not flight away from attachment, but rather an ever-purer participation in it...

Take none of this as a recipe. Instead of *thinking* about what I've said, try drinking it; let it intoxicate you, even as it blends with your own unfinished essay on the very same topic.

Deeper into now is the melody, my words suddenly but confetti vanishing into endless sky. Now I will ramble on in silence, my speech, inner and outer, overwhelmed by a green that is as wild as it is unreasonable...

4

True Center
And Its Chief Surrogate

The natural is what occurs when we are *already* happy, not depending on anyone or anything to produce our happiness. The evidence of such a condition is not to be found in opinion, belief, or emotional positioning, but in the quality of being — there may be secondary signs such as a luminosity and balance of eye, a capacity for easily cutting through reactivity, a depth of feeling that blends the powerful and the vulnerable, a love that is at ease with passion, and a compassion untainted by sentimentality, but the primary sign is a centeredness of being, a conscious abiding at one's core, that does not disappear with changes of mood or circumstance. Such centeredness may initially be held in place by some method or inner ritual of concentrated attention, but can only become firmly established when energy and attention are *naturally* devoted to it, free of all techniques and without any overriding motive of spiritual ambition.

Being centered in the physical, as in martial arts, is not enough; the centering impulse must also permeate the psychic, the emotional, the mental, and the spiritual. This is not about going within, as is the habit of the typical spiritual seeker, but about awakening. It is not the way of the introvert, the extrovert, or the convert, but the way of the lover, the one who can only keep embodying all that he or she is, regardless of the consequences. The lover looks not for refuge (inwardly or outwardly), but for revelation. The lover neither avoids suffering, nor unnecessarily reinforces it, knowing that to do either only drives one into compensatory activity. The true lover is a candle burning at both ends, solid as a pillar and transparent as a sigh — in him or her, individuality and surrender to the Source go hand in hand, flaming bright, merging deep, in heartfelt communion with each other, singing free the flesh of the lover, winging free the mind of the lover, saying nothing and teaching everything, until there is only unbound center, only Truth, only Eternal Unknowableness, forever inviting one and all to recognize it, to feel it, to be it...

True center emanates presence, not the presence of a strongly projected personality, which is known as charisma, but the presence of uninhibitedly embodied essence, ever disturbing the superficiality and psychological sleep of those nearby, ruthlessly, lovingly, and spontaneously exposing their most glaring delusions and perversions. And what is perversion? It is compulsive misalignment with the natural. It is misguided energy. It is loveless fire, its mind-frenzied heat driving us on and on, its sky but the ceiling of our hungriest thought. Perversion is a desperate coupling of mind and desire that promises deliverance or satisfaction, but that only erodes our integrity, gradually squeezing the life out of us.

By keeping us chronically hot, perversion distracts us from where we are frozen, often skilfully disguising itself as the natural. However, the natural, unlike the perverse, is not a suppression of being, nor is it a strategy designed to catalyze some sort of release. The natural is already free of the distress that seemingly necessitates such release, already free of the very motives that make perversion so attractive. With the natural, there still is suffering, but it is not *unnecessary* suffering; it is purification, it is empowerment of center, it is a deepening of the capacity to make good use of even the worst of circumstances, it is the freedom of not limiting joy to a particular location, condition, or mood...

For those who are deeply centered, there is no urge toward perversion, for they are already wonderfully consumed by the natural. They are too intimate with ecstasy to be impaled upon the peaks of pleasurable stimulation and distraction. Even if they engage in what appears to be perversion, at least in conventional terms, they are still doing what comes naturally — this is not licence, nor is it irresponsible, nor is it moral manipulation, so long as center is not being betrayed or abandoned. Of course, this is not in any way a rationalization for the behaviour of so-called spiritual teachers who, secretly or not so secretly, indulge in activities that only their stupidly undiscriminating devotees would view as non-abusive. Such teachers are not truly centered, or are lacking center in a particular area, especially that of emotion and sexuality. Unfortunately, all too many humans can't distinguish between the authentic and inauthentic — they only rely on belief or blind faith, reducing center to an *ideal*, or, more commonly, dream that they are *already* awake, already conscious, capable of free choice, capable of making real distinctions, when in fact it is only their intact *conditioning* that is making the choices. This is the melodrama that we compulsively act and re-enact, so thoroughly surrounding ourselves with its tension, escapism, anxiety, and delusion, that nothing else seems to exist, except for methodologies for pleasurable release.

Very few are those who have a center of being. It is not entirely accurate, however, to say that almost all humans have no center at all, for they are in possession of a parody of real center — egocentricity.

Ego, which can be defined as unconscious and obsessive identification with one's persona (or personality), is not a somebody, not even a something, but rather a *doing*, a process that mechanically refers to itself as a "me" — it is a habit gone to mind, a habit masquerading as "us." Ego sits not at the center of self, but at the center of a constellation of unexplored assumptions, beliefs, abstractions, and neurotic automaticities, constantly reinforcing itself through inflation, deflation, and psychological constipation, its efforts fueled by the unconscious granting of our attention to it.

Egocentricity has opinions just about everything, all of them claiming to be well-informed, when in fact they are only deformed, no more than the beepings of a robot, just arguments bereft of light, sucking energy and attention into that portion of the mind that spins out persona. Egocentricity's opinions and arguments are ardently defended by it, for they form its perimeter; to render them permeable, to let some Truth penetrate them, is to allow invasion, or change, a state of affairs that is anathema to the ego-centered, for without its assumptions held firmly in place, egocentricity loses face (which is everything to it).

Nevertheless, there is no point in trying to annihilate egocentricity. Ego is a disease of persona, needing only a deep inner cleansing, not with some brand of morality, but with open-eyed love and power. The result of such purification is not egolessness, except for an extremely rare few, but rather a radical shift in persona, so that it accurately reflects essence, letting it shine through, while lending it gracefully corresponding colour, idiosyncracy, and expression. A healthy persona is one that is not unconsciously identified with — it is the outer face of true individuality, the outward expression of one's uniqueness.

Persona as such does not control or mastermind sex, but gives it flavour. When sex goes deep, to where persona is obsolete, then persona must be let go of, or surrendered — to think or fantasize at such times (or even to cling to the intention to do so) only keeps persona in the action, thereby robbing sex of its possibility of being a seamless, mind-free communion with the totality of the other and with the Source. If ecstasy is thus bypassed through mind-fucking, however subtle, then there inevitably arises a craving for a lesser release; whatever stimulates us to the point of maximal pleasure, or to the point of a convincing illusion of ecstasy, becomes addictive for us. Again and again, we betray ourselves to ensure its repetition, churning out our engorged version of bliss, fucking ourselves into enervating oblivion, taking a brief vacation from the pain that we've created for ourselves through our very turning away from real ecstasy...

But if we do not thus turn away, if we do not thus remove ourselves from the truly nourishing, then there is no need to so manipulate ourselves, no need to pleasurably sedate ourselves, no need to corrupt ourselves with fantasy. Why fantasize when the real thing is right before us? Because we have made ourselves all but inaccessible to the real thing, and fantasy offers a compensatory substitute, a facsimile of the natural.

Egocentricity is nothing more than the personification of turning away from the natural. Letting it sit upon the throne of self only distresses us, making us ever more desperate for release. But if we will not leave our self-imposed prison, just how satisfying can any release within it be? The nightmare has only been interrupted, not undone, not awakened from. Shaking our heads, we settle for a life of self-entrapment, getting philosophical about our existential angst, complaining about our misfortune, scoffing not only at those who claim to have found a way out of the prison, but also at those who actually have found the way out!

Or perhaps we make-believe, in some metaphysical fashion, that we *are* out, reducing love, Truth, and sanity to mere ideals, gleefully or enthusiastically painting wings on our egocentricity and then calling it atman, soul, or Universal Self, feverishly pretending that we aren't pretending! The door is open, but only essence-centricity can approach it. The door is not within, nor without, but only here, existing *as* the heart of this very moment, swinging with your fullness of being, framing your unique adventure, inviting you through, *all* of you, including your persona, your suffering, your grief, your failure of nerve, your hunger, your joy, your everything...

5

Breakdown
Precedes Breakthrough

Breakdown precedes breakthrough. Losing face precedes facing the Truth. Confessing our inner whereabouts precedes locating our ecstasy. The broken wave knows the ocean, but only if it welcomes its breaking; put another way, we only have our heart's desire when we stop fighting the preparatory fire...

Letting go is the foundation of sanity, not a letting go that is but an avoidance of hurt, depth, and commitment, but rather a letting go blazing with naked feeling and empathetic sensitivity, a letting go intimate with grief and joy, a letting go that expands us enough to non-strategically include all that we are.

Let go, let go of bargaining for bliss, let go of the you who glamourizes letting go, let go of your evolutionary show, let go of your mistrust of letting go, let go of results, let go of acting awake, let go of doing it right, let go of master-minding your leap, let go now, let go throughout now, ever entering the realm of letting go without trying to let go, embracing rather than just trying to figure out its built-in paradoxical-ness...

Let go not to improve yourself, but to more fully be yourself. Let go not to reach sainthood, but to outshine every should. Let go not to transcend the mortal, but to embody its very heart. Let go not to escape to the Eternal, but to be the Eternal in time. Let go not to feel better, but to honour and live the ever-virgin Mystery, the Great Wonder and Womb of all history. Let go, let it go, let you go, and see what rises from the rubble. See what unsuspected glories sprout up from the ruins of what we took ourselves to be, and feel the sweetly dynamic surging of upstart green reaching and stretching for the light, splitting apart our concretized assumptions about ourselves...

Break down, fall apart, get messy, let your familiarity come unstrung, surrender your neurotic control, stop bargaining for guarantees, come disassemble your automaticities, scream and stream and howl and melt and shatter, letting all the bits and pieces swirl in the flood of your undamming.

What falls apart is not you, but only your surrogate authenticity. What falls apart is but your avoidance of your wholeness of being.

Let go fully, and allow yourself a truer foundation. Do not build anything prior to this; put aside your tools and impatience. Test your foundation by finding out whether or not you are still exploitable by others' expectations of you. If you are, then more breakdown is required.

Do it without whining or complaining. Abandon your audience, both inner and outer. Let go with open-eyed trust, knowing that you are permitting a necessary purification. Stop postponing the leap you know you are ready to take. Be willing to die. Be so ready to die that your life shines with full-bodied passion and ruthlessly loving compassion.

If you won't put everything on the line, what you have will *have* you. If you won't risk everything, you will risk ossifying the case of mistaken identity that you are now suffering.

Be dramatic if it helps. Be silent if it helps. Be outrageous if it helps. Do whatever you have to do, giving yourself full permission to uninhibitedly participate in your doing, however uncomfortable or painful it might be. Breathe more and more life into your trust, deliberately yielding to the organismic wisdom generated by the very momentum of your letting go, feeling your everything fountainbursting and streaming through you, until it's obvious that it *is* you, utterly and magnificently obvious, motivelessly spiralling out its own context, simultaneously celebrating both your individuality and your transcendental Identity...

Cry a river, rage a storm, do whatever it takes.

There are not higher stakes.

6

Egocentricity
& Essence-Centricity

Egocentricity is obsessive and unconscious identification with persona, whereas essence-centricity is conscious, full-blooded alignment with God, not the personified or idealized God of religion and metaphysical belief, but the God that is both the Source and Substance of all that is.

Egocentricity is a self-possessed knotting of attention, dressed up to look like individuality, ever perpetuating itself through exploitation of its environment, both inner and outer. Essence-centricity, on the other hand, is a spacious gathering and grounding of attention, providing both sufficient earth and sky for the full flowering of true individuality; it has no need to perpetuate itself, since it is already *knowingly* continuous with the Eternal.

Egocentricity projects itself everywhere, seeking its reflection, craving affirmation of its existence, madly cloning its patterns, like a tyrant who never has enough power — there is always something that might go wrong, something unknown, something threatening on the horizon, or from within. By contrast, essence-centricity *recognizes* itself everywhere, appreciating the diversity of its appearances, enjoying its sense of interrelatedness with all that exists; it is not afraid of changing form, nor of staying with a particular form, for it's *already* in embrace with the Undying Mystery that animates all forms.

Egocentricity clings to the past, and worries about the future, creating such distress for itself that it becomes addicted to remedial release, especially sexual. Essence-centricity, however, is rooted in the heart of the moment; release for it, including the sexual, is *not* an antidote for distress, nor an egoic consolation, but rather a full-bodied intensification of already-present joy.

Egocentricity is a habit gone to mind, a habit that insists on referring to itself as a "me," a habit that is but a personification of those entrapping assumptions that suppress Being. Essence-centricity *is* Being in action, already consciously embodied, already outdancing every egoic "me."

Egocentricity clings to facts, building self-serving mind-castles out of them, whereas essence-centricity can only express Truth, in fresh, unrehearsed correspondence to the conditions of the present moment.

Egocentricity is an attention-sucking cult of one. Essence-centricity is an individuated, attention-*giving* expression of the Unbound One.

It's either the spotlight, or God's Light...

7

There Are No Oscars
For Awakening

From a very early age, almost all of us, for reasons of psychophysical survival, learned to play a role (or roles) other than our true selves, literally embodying such primal artifice, automatically speaking *its* mind and fleshing out *its* scripted will, treating our native self either as though it weren't there, or as something to be mistrusted, something to subjugate, exterminate, imprison, or legislate into broken-spirited impotence.

Our skill at being other than ourselves, especially if in relatively consistent alignment with parental expectations and demands, was ordinarily rewarded, not only at home and at school, but also in the looming promises of a larger cultural sense, as epitomized by the Academy Awards for acting performance.

Our fascination with movie stars is precisely our fascination with the possibility of being immensely and gloriously rewarded for playing a designated role. Yes, we may crave escape from our role, but we usually are only looking for a better part, a juicier role, one that will more fully expose our talent, one that'll do a neon dance coast to coast, leaving all our critics rapturously comatose, especially those critics who have hurt us the most...

Nevertheless, we are haunted by our continuing self-betrayal, and burdened by our efforts to distract ourselves from it. How very practical it was initially, and how very addictive later on, in adolescence and "adulthood," to so thoroughly distract ourselves from the presence of such betrayal! How very, very tempting to have so much attention, even adulation, directed at our playing of our role, that we would be *immune* to our spirit-denial, pleasurably oblivious to the faraway cries of our native integrity of being! How intoxicatingly consoling! And how lonely.

A great actor embodies, without apparent effort, various archetypes of behaviour, with masterful timing and exquisitely appropriate shadings of expression, simultaneously conveying both the obvious and the subtle. His essence seems to shine through and fill out his acting; he appears to be happy, or fulfilled, in his role, however dark it might be. His happiness is, we imagine, the product of his acting talent and perseverance, and therefore, via extrapolation, *our* potential happiness seems to be available through *our* role, if we play it just right, and if our circumstances are sufficiently auspicious.

However, real happiness is *not* the product of anything — it is *already* present when we are true to ourselves. It is inherent to Being Itself. No acting is required, except that which spontaneously and naturally expresses the Truth of us. No one gets kudos for playing their true self; such "acting" transcends rehearsal at all levels, as well as all craving for approval.

There are no Oscars for awakening. There is no applause, and even if there were, it would not seduce our ear. When we are authentically ourselves, we no longer lust for recognition — we *give* attention, consciously and openly, rather than compulsively and automatically demanding it. Exploitation, whether of self or of others, is no longer an option for us. We are free of both hope and despair, defining ourselves neither through allegiance to, nor rebellion against, parental and cultural authority.

We outshine all stage fright (including that which eats at almost all, namely stage fright about performing what *cannot* be performed), again and again making room for all that we are, dark and light. Those who have shed their blinders will recognize us; others will turn from us, finding airtight excuses for doing so, not wanting to be reminded that they are pretending not to pretend. Our mere presence will be an offense to those who are dreaming they are awake, and it will also be an uncontrived invitation, a non-proselytizing welcoming, an open-heart stage, a gift, a challenge, and, eventually, a sacred *demand*. The superficial will no longer be an avoidance of the deep, but rather a playful expression of it, a brilliance of idiosyncratic surface in luminous resonance with its underlying currents. The Academy Awards may still occasionally parade across our television screen, but it will no longer fascinate us; it may even be watched for a while, but without sentimentality or cynicism, like colourful wrappings seen scuttling across a downtown parking lot on a windy Sunday...

When we are truly committed to the awakening process, then we can deliberately act, with no danger of mechanically identifying with any role in particular. Then acting is but Life-play, deeply potent improvisation, illumination-producing exaggeration, an unrehearsed celebration and mythic revelation, both ecstatic and grief-bright, of all that comes and goes. In the freedom of such acting, we glimpse and feel the All that does not come and go, the All that animates everything, the All that is not other than us.

True acting is beyond all re-acting. It is the sublime aesthetics, the outpouring flowering, the rainbowed embodiment, of Truth-telling, at once singing of both the Eternal and the temporal. True acting asks not for light, but effortlessly and motivelessly emanates light. It is gratitude in motion, overflowing with soulfire passion and prismatic wonder. It is the poetry of Truth, dancing us into and through the very heart of primal desire, dancing us through every us, dancing us round and round, in and out, up and down, until we are only here, right here, with no fear of fear, shining through our every appearance, deepening our colours through every interference, outdancing every would-be us that tries to claim the throne of Self...

8

Irony Undressed

Irony is intellectual exploitation of what appears to be contradictory or paradoxical; it presumes to point out some inconsistency or incongruity in this or that, its speech lightly veined with a tone of dry superiority. Irony's humour is arid and disembodied, moving a few masticatory muscles at most, leaving the trace of a faint yet unmistakably constipated smile.

Irony hides in its tower, buttoned-up to the neck, all sphincters under strict surveillance, looking down with carefully cultivated detachment for unreasonable behaviour among the masses, keeping an especially keen eye out for naked paradoxes. However, irony's knowledge of paradox is only superficial, a mere snapshot devoid of any holographic possibility. Irony may appear intelligent, but is not — it is far too specialized, far too partial and superficial, to have any real overview or depth of knowingness. Irony makes a meal out of facts and data, stuffing itself too full to have any room left for Truth; it doesn't see, and (because of its position) cannot see, that paradox is an essential and vital aspect of Truth (Truth being the very *heart* of paradox), for it is far too busy gathering facts for its argument.

Irony is not the logic of a clear mind, but of a mind bereft of conscious attention, a mind without *true* witness, a mind so thoroughly identified with that it masquerades as one's self. Those who indulge in irony are literally stuck in their headquarters, comforting themselves with cleverness, sarcasm, discrete voyeurism, and the sanitized rot of compulsive reasonableness.

Those who cling to irony are failed romantics; they have only replaced the sentimentality of romance with cynicism, and the false innocence of romance with false knowingness. Romance is illusory intimacy, fleshed-out with fantasy-manufactured sex rushes, whereas irony is illusory detachment, fleshed-out with wittily juxtaposed informational flushes. Both irony and romance are not only symptoms of a fragmentation of being, but are also compensations for such fragmentation, no more than sophisticated booby prizes.

Irony is cool, obsessively cool. It denies itself access to the heat of the awakening process, preferring imprisonment in its abstract apartment. And what happens when irony is flamed through and loosed? It becomes but wise, full-bodied humour, lovingly and forcefully cutting through human folly, with both mind-free passion and empathetic vulnerability for its subject matter. Thus does reasonableness laugh its head off, and wisdom outdance cleverness...

9

Responsibility
Is The Ground Of Freedom

Responsibility is self-generated, guilt-free accountability, an unrehearsed, naturally implanted capacity for responding practically, sensitively, and whole-heartedly to what is before us. Responsibility is not a slave of facts, but a servant of Truth; it is not bogged down by familiarity, nor by compulsive consistency, nor by the logic of reactivity, but is fresh and vital, centered in being rather than in mind, fluidly alert to the qualities and needs of the present moment.

Responsibility is earthy, but not dense — it both grounds and makes room for full participation in each of its moments. Specificity, subtlety, and sensitivity spontaneously comingle in the expression of real responsibility, so that balance, integrity, and love are restored to the situation at hand. Specificity is attention to detail, a keenly functional appreciation for logistics, structure, and pertinent information. Subtlety involves being attuned to two or more levels of being at the same time, with a corresponding accuracy of gesture, verbal content, vocal tone, and feeling. Sensitivity is simply empathetic consideration, a finely tuned emotional resonance, enriched with a vulnerability that's not a source of helplessness, but of strength. The synergistic blending of specificity, subtlety, and sensitivity is the body of responsibility, the earth from which it flowers.

The true taking of responsibility, at the level at which we are capable of doing so, is essential to maturation. Bypassing such responsibility, or being force-fed a facsimile of it, for so-called educational purposes, only stunts our growth, leaving us stranded in frozen childhood or adolescence, stuck in mere reaction, whether submissive or defensive, to the "responsibilites" of our culture, which are little more than deadening duties, taboo-enforcement, and robotic conformity, serving only the continuation of the society in which we "live."

What is ordinarily called responsibility is but joyless duty performed by one aspect of self, while another part plays saboteur or inertia-master, finding a dark pleasure in obstructing or frustrating the performer. This self-division, or fragmentation of self, is perfect breeding ground for guilt — again and again, we fall short of our "responsibilities," resenting their burdensomeness, pressure, and stress, blaming ourselves for doing so, or taking blame from others, obediently injecting ourselves with guilt, "good" resolutions, and more guilt, grimly treading water in our antiseptic cesspool, deifying whatever pleasurably distracts us from our stagnation, reducing freedom to the permission to do as we please within our self-entrapment.

Blame, however, is not equivalent to, nor part of, responsibility, contrary to the common and plaintive cry of "I'm responsible!", which is usually no more than the well-dressed side of self-blame, full of square-shouldered resignation and a suffocating suppression of being. Those psychotherapeutic and "New Age" movements that espouse "taking responsibility for creating one's reality" only teach their devotees to blame themselves for whatever isn't working in their lives, to fault themselves, and themselves *only*, for their failure to live up to the ideals of their particular movement. Blame sprouts from a morality imposed from without, a morality of simplistic right and wrong, a morality plagued by idealism, whereas responsibility stems from an ethic created not by society, nor by mind, nor by any "ism," but by deeply ingrained resonance with the Source of Life, a resonance bright with commonsense, open-eyed passion, and undiluted love.

Blame contracts us; responsibility expands us. Blame is a collapse of being; responsibility is *commitment* to being. Blame imprisons; responsibility frees. Blame teaches submission; responsibility teaches surrender, its surrender being a dynamic receptivity, a potent availability to the needs of the moment, a deep and graceful coordination of both the male and the female within us, luminous with center.

Responsibility need not be forced, for it is a natural function; to impose it on ourselves is to miss it. True responsibility is an expression of our wholeness of being, not of our submission to some external authority, even if such authority has set up camp behind our forehead.

Instead of taking responsibility, *be* responsible.

To do otherwise is but postponement. We know what we need to do. The intention to take the first necessary step is already with us, obvious to our hearts, obscured only by our addiction to our ideals, our desperate clinging to hope's phantoms. Nevertheless, we know there are no alibis, and we know it without thinking about it.

We know what we need to do, and, at the same time, we know what we need to undo...

10

Sentimentality & Cynicism

Sentimentality is secretly married to cynicism; sentimentality plays the softy, cynicism the hard-nose.

Sentimentality is a culturally acceptable perversion of real feeling, just as cynicism is a culturally acceptable perversion of real insight. Sentimentality produces an illusion of heart, cynicism an illusion of detachment; their positioning, mushy or clever, is unrelentingly rigid.

Sentimentality is the refuge of a damaged, compulsively nostalgic child, cynicism the refuge of an equally damaged, emotionally disembodied adolescent — both are but strategies to dull or minimize contact with what has been turned away from, namely one's core of being.

What sentimentality clings to, cynicism pushes away. Or so it seems. Look deeper, and notice how sentimentality actually pushes away what it so convincingly slobbers over, while cynicism in fact clings to what it so adroitly maligns or mocks.

Their marriage vow is to not appear in public together. They leave the lights off when they copulate. Their child moans in a soundproof cell.

Both parents suspect that all is not well, but merely continue fleshing out their automaticities, consoling themselves with regular doses of romanticism and irony, dutifully maintaining their mutual hell...

11

Working With Criticism
(a talk)

It is important to understand what criticism is, what its function is, what its surrogates are. Criticism cannot be healthy unless it is given by one who has center, by one who is in conscious contact with their core of being — not by one who *thinks* they're in such contact, but by one who *is*. Otherwise, criticism cannot be healthy, truly healthy; when it is, it is accidentally so, a matter of the right thing being done for the wrong reason. For example, someone, asleep to their true nature, their depths and so forth, may have an apparently good heart, may be a seemingly loving person, may well manifest action that supports this, but they could just as easily, and often do, become involved in activities that are not loving at all — on the one hand, they can love up their children with a benign sentimentality, and on the other hand, patriotically send them off to some misbegotten war, or to some kind of educational training that is little more than gross indoctrination into a robotic society.

So-called constructive criticism, when delivered by those without center, is patronizing, invulnerable, *compulsively* reasonable and, above all, *controlling*, ever seeking to subjugate its recipient to a morality derived from mind, a morality devoid of real illumination! So-called constructive criticism is usually presented in a manner that is cloyingly parental, suffocatingly parental, terminally nice. Such criticism is hiddenly cruel (the flip side of niceness being meanness) because it is not empathetically aligned with its target — it is only apparently empathetic, apparently concerned, apparently considerate. It is actually only a syruped plea to not rock the boat, to not make waves, unless such waves are made in a socially prescribed manner, or in a manner approved by one's peers (or cultic co-participants). Constructive criticism, when delivered by the centerless, is actually *destructive*, utterly destructive to the spirit.

It is simply the smiling face of destructive criticism.

All criticism coming from those who have no intimacy with their
depths is ultimately harmful, for it doesn't serve the well-being of the
other, not deliberately — when it does hit the mark, it's accidental. It
could just as easily miss. Its accuracy is of information, not of spirit,
not of context, not of heart. The intent of typical criticism is to get
whomever it is aimed at to stay in line, to conform, to neurotically
conform. Such criticism is without love, no matter how much syrup it is
mixed with, no matter how benign its parental overtones. Unfortunately, very few people recognize the difference between healthy and
unhealthy criticism, unhealthy criticism being both typically constructive *and* destructive criticism.

Healthy criticism is consciously delivered, illuminated by spirit, friendly
in its occasional ferociousness, ruthless in its love. Skilfully given, it is
capable both of empathetic subtlety and extreme penetration and
force. It is *not* judgmentalness, judgmentalness simply being a species
of criticism devoid of light. Illuminate judgmentalness, and you have
true insight. Such insight, when accompanied by correspondingly
resonant gestures of body and tone of voice, *works* — it is inherently,
empathetically aligned with its recipient, even if it is harshly given.
Even if it is given with tremendous force!

Those who are in long-term recoil from parental rejection and disap-
proval shrink in the face of criticism, healthy or unhealthy. They all too
easily identify with what is being criticized. They shrink, making
themselves smaller and smaller before the looming size of their apparent attacker. Others seem impervious to criticism, capable of deflecting
it with ease. However, such people are not mature relative to the
reception of criticism, but are simply defended; they have merely
shrunk themselves in spirit, having already retreated into their shell,
removing their soft parts to the darkest, innermost spirals of their
calcified defence. Others inflate themselves when faced with criticism,
but their heart is already deflated, already collapsed, all but inaccessible. Very, very few people know how to receive criticism, simply
because very few people have center. Few are those who are passionately committed to cultivating true center, to reclaiming their native
integrity of being. Very few are inclined this way. And when criticism
comes their way, what do they do?

First of all, they don't do something that has been thought out before-
hand. They don't rehearse their response. They don't stand there and

absorb criticism like a sponge, nor do they necessarily deflect it — they *feel* it, in the moment when it is given. They don't expect the deliverer of it to always look loving — they don't need the reassurance that they are being loved, because they are *already* responsible for being loving, for remaining open to their capacity to love. Therefore, they receive criticism in a spontaneous, improvisational manner. They may even deflect it, or they may get angry if the criticism is being delivered in a cruel or unconscious or clearly reactive manner. Or they may simply remain passive before it, allowing themselves to be penetrated by it, permeated by it, effected, moved to tears, to weeping, to deep vulnerability, to hurt, to healing laughter. They receive healthy criticism as a gift, even if the gift is an arrow to the heart, a Zen blow to the side of the head, a blast to the belly, a shove into the unknown, a rough shove...

They receive it all as a gift, but not with the obeisance and disgusting obsequiousness of the devotee, forever flat on their faces thanking and thanking and thanking the Master for such grace. No, they simply are *grateful* for healthy criticism, and they show their gratitude by receiving it, by making good use of it, by honouring the one who gives it, by recognizing the risk that person is taking in delivering it. And when unhealthy criticism comes their way, they don't submit to it — they stand their ground like a tree in a storm, or they leave. Again and again, they surrender to healthy criticism, letting themselves be broken by its intensity. They allow its challenging insight to wound them, to tear them open where they are closed, so that they are nakedly exposed in such places to light, to sanity, to rejuvenation, to love. Thus are they again and again restored to a richer, deeper balance of being, a truer alignment with God.

There is no recipe for giving and receiving criticism. If there is no center, no commitment to center, criticism is unhealthy, even when it appears healthy, even when it is of value. Then it is simply coincidentally, accidentally valuable. Those who moan about forcefulness of criticism, chronically whining about "Why can't you say it more softly? Why can't you be more gentle?" only want to *control* the force, the power, coming their way; they want to dilute it, to rob it of its passion, especially its male passion. They don't realize that by denying criticism its force, its potent fullness, they are reducing the possibility that they could grow from such criticism — they merely *think* that if they hear the content of criticism being gently voiced, they will somehow grow from it. Bullshit! They won't grow from it, but will at *best* become enthusiastic about it for a few days, perhaps making resolutions to change, giving themselves an assignment or two to alter something in themselves that was being addressed by their criticizer. But then after a few days, when their mood changes, and circumstances alter the picture, they forget, conveniently forget, rationalizing their way back into what they knew needed to be changed.

Criticism requires subtlety, sensitivity, attention to detail and context, courage, empathy, and also the willingness to use one's sword, to go for the guts, to get to the heart of the matter, to be uncompromisingly ruthless at times, to be blunt — this of course does not mean to always deliver the full force of one's criticism to another. To do so, out of some misguided notion of honesty, would be very insensitive, grossly inconsiderate. There is a right time for force, even a right time for harshness, just as there is a right time for softness and artful inquiry. If one is angry while one is giving criticism, and the anger is clearly not reactively based, then it ought to be given with passion, open-faced passion, given with such intensity that it must yield to what underlies it, to all the vulnerability, the old hurt, the longing for intimacy, and so on, that is behind it, so that a fluid intimacy can be reestablished...

But most people are terrified of angry criticism. They withdraw from its heat, they throw dirt at it, they want to smother it, to control it, to remove themselves from its flames. All one can do is stay in touch with center and simultaneously yield to the storminess, the brilliance, the sheer wildness of authentic criticism when it is fiery. Other times, when criticism is soft, cloudlike, feathery, presented with delicious lightness and humour, one must still let it in, like earth receiving rain. One must be willing to receive healthy criticism however it is given, and to respond appropriately to it, whether with anger, laughter, tears, whatever, taking it as gift, a gift that asks only to be welcomed and unwrapped, a gift that will all too soon wither and die if it is not made good use of...

12

Teasing As A Psychospiritual Martial Art

Real teasing is a sublime yet wondrously visceral skill, a spontaneous amalgam of accuracy, love, wit, and multi-dimensional humour, that catalyzes expansion, or at least potently presents expansion as a very accessible option. Such teasing does not just work away at a weak spot, but tunnels down into the very *roots* of it, exposing it to sudden bolts of light, with a dexterity as much of emotion as of mind — this requires not only a fluid sensitivity and a capacity to create instant theatre, but also a deep love of both force and subtlety.

True teasing is a psychospiritual martial art, fierce as it is tender, both pantherine and clownish, firmly yet playfully balanced, adept with both watercolour brush and sledgehammer. It is outrageous without being overdone, subtle without being obscure or devious, and wild without being savage.

Without teasing, we tend to get overwhelmed by or lost in drama; skilful teasing (if we are receptive enough to it) so richly exaggerates our habitual dramatics that we are relieved of their seriousness, our commitment to their script suddenly but a laughing matter, a happy embarrassment, an unveiled absurdity.

Real teasing is an act of love, a reinforcer of intimacy, a delight of exquisite timing, a vibrant improvisation designed to make more room for joy and sanity. It may wear a clown's mask and carry a rapier, but its heart is out-front. However, this doesn't necessarily mean that it is always friendly — its love is too strong to worry about looking good. It is not out to snare approval or applause, nor to keep things tidy; sometimes its jabs and probes really hurt, but only to draw attention to repressed or neglected aspects of us.

Teasing, when delivered skilfully, pulls down the pants of our neurotic rituals, in full view of at least one witness, outer or inner.

It is the leavening of healthy criticism, efficiently and aesthetically deflating our efforts to be somebody special, leaving us, if we intelligently receive its lucid troublemaking, vulnerable and a little wiser, more firmly reestablished in our natural uniqueness, lighter yet more solid, stronger yet more flexible, unambiguously shining through our every role...

13

Hope Is
Nostalgia For The Future

Hope is no more than despair taking a crash course in positive thinking. Uproot hope, and you will have also uprooted despair; pain may still be present, but it will no longer merely be something to flee or fix, but rather just the periphery of an intensity through which we must pass.

Hope is bravely smiling doubt. Its promises only seduce us into postponing Now, cheerfully greening our deserts with peptalk oases, plastic shade trees, and mind-induced spasms of enthusiasm.

Hope is a hit, a heart-tease, a neuronal rush, a cleancut upper, a storybook romance with Later.

Hope doesn't see, and hope doesn't free. There is no hope for hope. Who really needs its antiseptic smile and stupidly patriotic style? Who really needs its misguided reading of the past, and its misguided loyalty to the future?

Hope murders ecstasy, by *addicting* us to possibility. Where hope ends, we begin. When the lights are left on, there's no need to grope for hope.

Hope is but nostalgia for the future.

14

The Beginning Of Work On Oneself

Almost all of what is referred to as work on oneself is not, but is only *preparation* for work on oneself. Such preparation is effort, sustained effort; it is a testing, an utterly essential testing wherein one encounters, after a brief honeymoon with initial breakthroughs, one's resistance to awakening, integration, ecstasy, and true responsibility. This resistance must not be avoided, whether through enthusiasm, mental affirmation, emotional dissociation, or any other kind of counter-effort, but rather must be *directly* faced and consciously passed through, not to escape it, nor to somehow annihilate it, but to liberate its energies for the process of becoming *fully* human.

Only when this step has been taken over and over again, with a resulting maturity epitomized by a significant lessening of reactivity, can work on oneself actually begin. Such work cannot proceed without a steady and pure foundation — profound commitment is necessary, not a forced or spiritually ambitious commitment, but a natural commitment, one that arises because *all* other options no longer can seduce us. This has nothing to do with promises, nor with "good" resolutions, nor with hope. It is an act of totality, an act rooted in one's core of being, an act from which there is no turning back, without severe damage to oneself.

Real work on oneself is both effort and non-effort. The effort, unlike in the preparatory stage, is secondary to, and arises from, one's non-effort, or capacity for relaxed alertness. If this were reversed, if effort were still primary, then discipline would all too easily obstruct the work through its very form (and goal-fixation), rather than supporting it — discipline here is not about self-improvement (nor any other egocentric manipulation of self), but is about maintaining a conducive environment, both inner and outer, for the awakening process. Put another way, work on oneself happens by itself, but only when we are truly ripe for it, swollen with inner light and unbound energy, overgrown with longing — this is *not* just passivity in the ordinary sense, but is a dynamic waiting, an extremely potent receptivity, a spacious and sensitive inner listening, out of which what is necessary makes itself obvious. Implicit in this is a trust of a sort unknown to almost all...

One must become capable of assuming this trust, and of living it fully, not as an act of faith or devotion, but because there is, after a certain point, nothing else to do. This point marks the beginning of work on oneself.

15

When Effort Transcends Trying

True effort, or essence-centered doing, arises from the fecund brilliance of lucid non-effort, which is not to be confused with any sort of laziness or inertia, but rather is to be recognized and felt through its vibrantly receptive ease, its relaxed yet alert availability, its dynamic stillness and juicy spaciousness, abundantly pregnant with fluid, eminently practical blueprints for appropriate action — such *naturally* unfolding directives are formed not in correspondence to our neurotic inclinations, but instead to the energies and needs of our current situation. Thus does reactivity yield to responsiveness, and rehearsal to a thoroughly grounded spontaneity.

When most, if not almost all, people are supposedly doing nothing, they are endogenously comatose, crippling themselves so as to avoid all participation, or, more commonly, they are actually busying themselves with the chatter, polarizations, and scenarios of their thinking minds, mechanically ricocheting between and identifying with various cognitive associations, repetitiously occupying and filling themselves with a bewildering smorgasbord of inner reruns, again and again propagandizing themselves with obsolete assumptions, ever burying themselves in their unresolved past, or in their future (which is little more than an extrapolation of their past, whether hope-injected or despair-filled).

True non-effort requires preparation — the plowing and working of its soil is hard labour, a sustained, muscular effort of a kind very different than that of essence-centered effort. Because of the usual beginner's unillumined condition, the work that must be done *before* authentic non-effort can come into being is not only inevitably endarkened and frustratingly muddy in intent, plagued with well-meaning misdirection, but is also of real use only when it's consistently harnessed to the will of a true teacher (or, much more rarely, solely to the will of one's core of being)...

An almost blind, yet heartfelt gutsiness and faith keeps the effort, the soil-breaking, moving in the most fruitful direction until some degree of awakening is *stably* established, at which point the teacher, if possessed of integrity, pulls back without any diminishment of intimacy, skilfully allowing a psychological weaning to occur, so that the student might more fully ripen into the domain of true non-effort, rather than simply becoming more and more addicted to the teacher. Such emerging maturity does not necessarily mean that the teacher is no longer of any use, but that the teacher can now be made even better use of by the student.

The lover openly embodies both effort and non-effort, not divorcing passion and witnessing, but joining them in holy lust, falling neither into the trap of conventional passivity and indifference, nor into that of compulsive activity and rigid possessiveness, thereby avoiding the spiritual diseases of both East and West. The extremes of Taoist "non-work" and Gurdjieffian "work" are not indulged; the non-method obsessiveness of Khrishnamurti enthusiasts and the method-addicted fanaticism of various yogas and psychotherapies are bypassed. The lover does not force or seduce others into a system, but nor does he or she make a virtue out of non-interference — strong, fiery action is just as valued as sublime stillness. What must be done, however distasteful or unpopular, is unequivocally embraced and allowed to emerge full-hearted and fully-armed from the womb of non-effort, spontaneously blending both directness and subtlety.

Ordinary effort is but trying, trying, and more trying, chronically in doubt of its commitment, burdened by egocentric survival motives. On the other hand, true effort carries and is carried by its own organismic commitment; its imperatives are not self-enclosed, but are in deeply felt resonance with its environment, serving not the will of our slumber, but that of our spirit-awakening.

Trying carries within itself a largely unacknowledged counter-effort — that's why it's such a sweaty, anxiety-riddled activity. "I tried" is not only a statement of good intentions, but, more importantly, of self-dividedness and self-sabotage. Trying is but the ambitious doing of a *piece* of us, whereas real effort is action arising from our totality, however specialized its branchings might be. Don't try; simply *do*. Don't try to not try, but rather make room for the coming together of all that you are, permitting a natural doing to arise and emerge from the vibrant fertility of such reunion of being.

To try is to lie; to naturally do is to be true. Undo the knot of your trying, undo it without hurrying and without wasting time. Untie it and breathe it bright, letting your everything flood the you who's addicted to such a knotting of being, the you who needs not annihilation, nor spiritual consolation, nor more shrinkwrapped isolation, but love, welcome, and transmutation, not to mention celebration. It's worth the effort...

Part II

**Releasing Sex
(And Everything Else)
From The Obligation
To Make Us Feel Better**

16

Introduction:
The Abuse Of Sex

The abuse of sex is so pervasive and so deeply ingrained as to go all but unnoticed, except in its more lurid or perverse extremes. Even more removed from awareness is our aversion to truly exploring and illuminating the whole matter of human sexuality, not clinically, nor according to a particular philosophy, nor in any other kind of isolation, but in the context of our *entire* being. Sex cannot be crystallized out from the rest of our experience — it must be seen, felt, and lived in full-bodied resonance with *everything* we are and do, so that it is not an act of separation and egoic consolation, but rather a celebration of wholeness, a mutually ecstatic intensification of intimacy, an already-happy, already-unstressed being-to-being meeting and greeting, asking only for unrestrained nakedness and empathetic joy...

The abuse of sex, whether by the hedonistic, the prudish, the obsessively analytical, the promiscuous, the monogamous, the troubled, the lonely, the spiritually ambitious, or the unhappy, is a matter of repetitiously misdirected energy. Some fuck away their anger, draining themselves of the very force that could, if channeled with potent sensitivity, break through barriers to intimacy. Some mind-fuck, busily consuming and rekindling genital excitation through compulsive thinking and fantasizing, again and again losing themselves in the titillating dramatics of their engorged minds. Some deify erotic sensation and stimulation, making sure their sex center is always open for business, exhaustively advertising their availability. Some paint wings on their ego, calling it atman or soul or Universal Self, and try, in yogic or meditative fashion, to use their sexual energy as fuel for their illusory flight. Some mistake the rushing of sexual passion into their emotional center for love, and get romantic, abandoning themselves in their irresponsible dissolution of their boundaries, fucking the brains out of hope, making sentimental poetry out of swooning chestfuls of lust. Some (most, in fact) fuck away what they can of their fear, anxiety, doubt, and insecurity, thereby reducing sex to a safety-valve (or psychological garburetor) for the release of distress, using eroticism, pornography, fantasy, and whatever else works to keep the valve open, or at least lubricated...

Some flee sex, some force-feed it, some crush it, some never let it rest, some marry it to their minds, some feel guilty about it, some brag about it, some hedge it in, some flaunt it, some sell it, some buy it, some prosecute it, some wear it, some spiritualize it, some sit on it, some shit on it, but almost all abuse it, forcing it to do other than its true work, repeatedly binding it to the chore of making us feel better, whether through pleasurable distraction, stress-discharge, neurotic sublimation, or romantic delusion.

Sex, however, is not meant to be a slave, nor an all-purpose salve, nor a sedative. Its ongoing misuse is not only harmful in terms of enervation, degradation, and deception, but also in terms of our potential for awakening to our true condition — if we are habitually fucking away our passion (especially that of stress-generated sexual craving) or tying it up in rituals of mind, then we are left emptied of, or marooned from, the very energy we need to spark and stabilize our realization of who we really are. In other words, our Life-energy in such a circumstance is automatically committed to something other than the awakening process, and will be until we somehow interfere...

At the same time, repressing or rising above our sexuality, as in certain so-called spiritual practices, does not work — there may be an increased clarity of perception, a heightened awareness, sensations of bliss, and so on, but, more importantly, there is a dissociation from feeling, from passion, from lust, an avoidance of fully embodying oneself, a recoil from human intimacy that is but one more confession, however sophisticated, of the suppression of being that plagues just about everyone, that ubiquitous fragmentation of self that's looking *not* for reunion, but for immunity from the very pain inherent to it.

When we tap into an experience that brings us some relief or pleasure, we tend to cling to it, to exploit it as much as we dare; we become, to varying degrees, addicted to its repetition. The distress created by such addiction only intensifies our hunger for the desired experience. Thus does love die, trampled beneath our craving for release from the very distress generated by such craving! In short, we are inclined to set up dependency-relationships with *whatever* seems to make us feel better, or safer, or more secure — we make our well-being dependent upon whether or not we are having a particular experience, simultaneously resenting our dependency and compensating for it by presenting ourselves, directly or indirectly, as pillars of independence (or simply by pretending that we aren't addicts).

This self-generated bondage is perhaps most commonly seen in our sexual intent and action. Far too often, we use sex to feel happy/whole, instead of doing what we need to do in order to feel, prior to sex, *already* happy/whole, so that sex is a sharing of our happiness, a juicy celebration of our wholeness, a gift of overflow, a deeply nourishing and rejuvenating giving and receiving. Using sex to make ourselves feel better only unnecessarily burdens our sexuality, knotting it up with the job of easing our distress and tension.

Sex can be used to illuminate the roots and inner workings of our distress, but only if it is engaged in consciously (which does not mean playing detached witness, but rather participating with uninhibited, full-bodied, open-eyed passion and vulnerability). Not many of us want to do this, especially if sex-release is our primary method for bringing about "good" feelings and tension-relief. Why should we threaten what seems to be such a dependable outlet, such a quick and easy pleasure-source? We may not want to risk interrupting or deflating our genital exercise. We may not want to see our sexual behaviour stripped of its mechanicalness, its lies, its manipulativeness, its desperation, its mind-connection. We may not want to see what we are *actually* up to during sex, aside from pleasurably stimulating ourselves. We may not want to acknowledge what our minds are doing during sex, let alone our bodies!

To the point: If we pay conscious attention to ourselves and our partner in the midst of sex (which does not mean *thinking* about what's going on!), we will gradually see the underpinnings of our suffering with remarkable clarity, as well as our craving to escape from that suffering. We will see how we are abusing ourselves, how we are misrepresenting ourselves, how we are imprisoning ourselves — we will literally catch ourselves in the act, recognizing that what we do sexually is but an *exaggeration* of what we do when we aren't being sexual. However reluctantly, we will eventually see through our craving for orgasm, realizing that when we make orgasm the goal, we only screw ourselves. We will no longer merely exploit the heat of sex's fire, but will make use of its light, understanding with our entire being that sexual sanity and joy is impossible without a corresponding sanity and joy in the rest of our life.

Sexual freedom is not the freedom to be heterosexual or homosexual or bisexual or asexual, nor is it the freedom to masturbate, to fantasize, to be promiscuous or celibate or flirtatious or morally erect, limp, liberal, or silent. Sexual freedom is not about permission or rules or morality, but is the freedom of awakening, not a dry, desireless awakening, but a passionate, fleshy, heartfelt awakening. It is no turning away from or rising above Life, nor is it indulgence of lust. It is not conventional freedom, which is but the freedom of an animal to move unhindered through its cage, but rather the freedom of unchained Life, brilliant in its feeling, vibrant in its love and empathy, pure in its force and in its subtlety, true in its shallows and in its depths, lusty with the sacred, tender with the ridiculous, effortlessly intimate, unbound to any ideal, again and again arising when joy is made the foundation, rather than the goal. There is no use, however, in trying to embody such freedom as long as we persist in living in artificial light. The impulse to awaken must be contacted, and its imperatives implicitly obeyed, no matter what our mood or circumstance. Only then does our integrity bloom, and our freedom possess us...

When we stop depending on sex (or anything else) to make us feel better, we stop making a problem out of dependency itself, finding in ourselves a strength that is utterly *unthreatened* by dependency or attachment, a strength that both serves the ripening of our individuality, and our communion with the Source of All. We don't hide our need. We let go more and more easily, without withdrawing from intimacy. We cease protecting our hearts. Our way becomes not the way of the introvert, the extrovert, or the convert, but that of the lover.

The essays that follow are about sex, and therefore about passion, love, intimacy, spirit, ecstasy, and wakefulness, as well as about the turning away from these and their resulting substitutes, all the diseased surrogates that animate our entrapping dreams. Do not read this or what follows politely — take your clothes off, get messy, get turned on, get turned off, get turned loose, be outraged, be eased, be undone, let your deadening familiarity come unstrung. Come join me, come read me, come feel me, come steal yourself back, come breathe yourself sane, come take the kernel of what I'm saying and lustily crack it with your teeth, letting its juices ruin your shirt or blouse, letting its currents stream down or up or around or wherever you are, drawing you out, until you are filled to overflowing with your own awakening shout. So let us now more fully enter the domain of sex, naked and curious, relaxed and alert, already a little juicy...

17

The Anatomy Of Eroticism

Eroticism is the psychophysical commercialization of the sexual impulse. Just about everything that catalyzes, or promises, sexual stimulation and satisfaction is but an object for its calculating eye, something to buy a share in, something to package and profitably replicate, something to hot-wire genitalia and thoughts to, something to form a dependency-relationship with...

Eroticism is obsessive interest in sexual opportunity or possibility. It makes an idol out of pleasurable excitation, or charge, thus bringing about addiction to whatever maximizes, or once maximized, such charge — this intensifies not only our distress, but also our urge for orgasmic release. However, such release, whatever its inner advertising, is neither ecstasy nor liberation, but only exaggerated relief, a mere discharge of the *branchings* of distress, a fucking-away of tension (erotic and otherwise), akin to the relief felt when an extremely tight pair of shoes is at last removed. Repeatedly putting the shoes back on in order to later have a pleasurable release is the essence of eroticism.

Nevertheless, eroticism remains a very popular refuge for the disturbed, who compulsively use it as a mechanism for facilitating the discharge of distress via sex — it keeps us in near-constant heat, neurotically available for copulatory rituals, inner and outer, just as tightly bound to sexual possibility as anxiety is to threatening possibility. Eroticism, with our easily-bought cooperation, keeps our sex center open for business as a psychological garburetor and tension-dump, as well as an entertainment complex bulging with steamy distraction and soporific consolation.

Eroticism is but unilluminated lust polluted by fantasy, kept on the burner by our very urge for release from its contractedness, misguided suggestiveness, and underlying desperation. Again and again we mechanically fuck away our craving to fuck, emptying ourselves of our eroticized craving even as we strengthen and complicate its roots, ever looking for a *better* pair of tight shoes.

Thus do we crave getting rid of the intensity of desire itself, feeling ourselves unable to tolerate its fleshed-out presence, even as we force-feed it again and again, even as we think it full, even as we mind-fuck it into inflationary frenzy.

With numbing regularity, we eroticize ourselves into a position where we have to have some sort of release, some sort of orgasmic consolation, some sort of semi-blissful sedation, which only deprives us of the very energy we need in order to really investigate the source of our distress...

Eroticism promises happiness, but real sex *begins* with happiness.

Eroticism is but visceral-mental technology for tension-release through fucking; real sex is spontaneous play, needing *no* distress for its art, needing no preconceived stimulation for its passion, needing no fantasy and no strategy for its joy. Sex for awakened lovers may include intense stimulation at times, but this is created not by friction or conflict, but only arises as an utterly natural byproduct of their love-play. They *already* feel good; they are not expecting sex to make them feel good. They are not suppressing their being and making a *goal* out of release, for they are already released, already at ease, already in embrace with the heart of their desire, already consciously consumed by their passion's fire, already in love...

By reinforcing the *must* in lust, eroticism cheapens desire, stripping it of its spontaneity and expansiveness, injecting it with compensatory fantasy. As such, eroticism is an abuse of imagination. If we need to fantasize in order to have "good" sex, then we are not truly interested in sex, but rather in a mind-game whose purpose is but to *maximize* pleasurable release. Sex doesn't need mind in order to function, and will in fact not work, not flow fully and freely, if thoughts and fantasies are allowed to intrude into and dominate its domain. The only use of mind in sex is that of psychic communion between lovers; this requires an expansiveness of mind, whereas eroticism is but contraction of mind, crawling with pornographic abstraction.

And what happens to eroticism when sex is no longer gone to mind?

What becomes of eroticism when happiness is not the goal, but the foundation? It becomes but the playful expression of desire, its face that of longing, not a tense, ambitious longing, but an ecstatic, open-eyed longing to share one's depths with another through flirtatiousness and sexplay that's as loving as it's lusty, as subtle as it's juicy, as free of mind as it is full of wonder. The point is *not* to eradicate eroticism, but to illuminate and purify it, to allow it to be free of desperation and egocentricity, so that it can outgrow itself, becoming but available Life-energy, cutting new, life-giving channels, ever reestablishing our embrace with our Eternal Lover...

18

Masturbation
Revisited & Ungripped

Though masturbation is commonly thought of as a solitary act, it actually pervades almost all sexual encounters, however well-disguised it might be. It is the meat and potatoes of fucking, dressed up with wine, lip-smacking sauces, extra-low lighting, and a sizzling overdose of mind. Masturbation is the engine pumping away beneath the glistening, just-polished hood, the red-faced highschool dropout anonymously toiling inside the factory of romantic delusion, the bulging yet forgotten furnace in the day-dream mansion, the manual transmission of erotic compulsion.

Masturbation is hands-on expertise in burning up the outermost branchings of distress through genital excitation and release — it is what we do when we, feeling contracted, disturbed, anxious, lonely, bored, doubtful, or otherwise out of balance, try to alter our condition via sexual stimulation and climax, seeking to feel better or to console ourselves through such an exercise, manipulating ourselves into a less than honourable discharge of Life-energy. Not only do we fuck *ourselves*, but we *fuck away* much of the very energy needed to fuel our reaching and truly seeing the roots of our distress, as so eloquently expressed in the epithet "Fuck me dead!"

The word "fuck" has many meanings beside that of copulatory activity, all of them pithy articulations of what we are *actually* up to during sex, revealing through both their content and their feeling the twisted roles we force sex to play, so that we might be pleasurably distracted from what we must face if we are to become fully human.

Throw all the meanings of "fuck" together, and you'll have an eloquent collage of the slave labour to which sex has been sentenced by all those who have chosen sedation over awakening.

Friction and fantasy stoke the furnace, and upstairs the "lovers" sweat and fret through their neurotic script, mistaking sensation for feeling, sentimentalized excitation for love, and mutual masturbation for intimacy. When the furnace gives out or malfunctions, despair sets in, perhaps inspiring a call to the repairman (sex therapist, psychiatrist, counsellor) or a fervent dip into the latest sex manual. A few repairs are made, a few new beliefs may be swallowed, a few techniques may be recommended — the symptoms are removed, "fixed," numbed, rationalized, or rearranged, but are rarely ever seen for what they really are.

And who wants to really question masturbation? Not condemn it, not praise it, not buy or sell it, but *truly* question it, until its roots are clearly illuminated. To see what masturbation is at essence is to see what we are doing with our entire lives; it is to see the extent to which we exist only to gratify and distract ourselves; it is to see that almost all of us are asleep most of the time, only dreaming that we are awake; it is to see that masturbation consoles us *within* the dream, literally robbing our awakening impulse of its force. One who is in the dream can *only* masturbate, however romantic the setting. True love-making can occur only outside the dream — it is an ecstatic dance of flesh, spirit, and unrestrained feeling that very few know, but that all intuit as a possibility. Awakening from the dream has much to do with becoming *expansively* sensitive to one's distress, so sensitive that it is impossible to postpone taking the leap that one intuitively knows one has to take, however alien it might seem, however frightening, however antisocial, however risky, for it is far more of a risk to one's being to not take such a leap...

Masturbation is friction with a payoff, friction that comes through, friction that both relieves and soporifically distances us from emotional and psychological constriction, without the slightest illumination. Whether the lights are on or off, masturbation is done in the dark. With very few exceptions, it is a confession of loneliness, as well as a strategy for getting rid (at least temporarily) of the sensation of loneliness. As such, it is a fucking away of the force needed for real relationship, or intimacy, thus reinforcing the very loneliness for which it seems to be a solution.

In the Victorian era, masturbation was viewed with righteous horror; various "authorities" announced that its use would lead to insanity, hair upon the palms, blindness, and so on. Nowadays, it is increasingly fashionable to praise or feel good about masturbation; sex therapists extoll its virtues, enthusiastically encouraging its use, recommending it as an excellent means of arousal, not seeing that if passion must be artificially or strategically induced, then it is but a camouflaging of the need to *directly* face whatever it is we are doing that prevents the arising of real passion, or ecstasy. Sex therapists seem to be blind to the fragmentation of being, the psychospiritual sleep, the craving to feel better, the obsession with orgasm, the excruciating loneliness, that generates masturbatory inclination. A further confirmation of their blindness is their recommendation of using fantasy during sex, if it makes you "feel good," or if it helps you remain in a state of sexual *excitation*. The assertion that such fantasy use is healthy and natural is pure bullshit, perfumed with a liberalism that is but the knee-jerk opposite of the conservatism of earlier times.

It is true that masturbation and sexual fantasizing may be of some use to those who are deeply repressed sexually — a taboo is broken through, or challenged, and things get rolling at a very low level, the wheels leaving the mud-trap, the engine turning over, the gear-shift at last in one's own hands. However, the us who now sits in the driver's seat very soon no longer needs the push that unstuck our vehicle; if we keep resurrecting it, or returning to it, or depending on it, we will only be spinning our wheels, which is the very stuff of typical sex, or masturbation. To make a virtue out of masturbation and sexual fantasy is, in almost all cases except for those of extreme repression, utterly irresponsible, but if sex therapists didn't do so, they'd soon be out of business, no longer able to exploit people's craving to feel better via sexual stimulation, or else they would awaken to a more life-giving approach to "helping" others (and themselves).

So-called problems like impotence, frigidity, fetishism, and porno-graphic obsession are *not* sexual problems, but problems of feeling, of being, symptoms of self-fragmentation, dramatic byproducts of mis-taken identity — they are not to be "fixed," but rather to be seen and felt by our entire being, viewed in the context of our totality. When this is done, and done with passion and liberated attention, our "pro-blems" naturally mutate into available Life-energy, uncommitted to any and all loveless intentions. Impotence, for example, becomes not superstud-fuck-all-night capacity, nor on-call erectile service, but liber-ated male force, as sensitive as it is powerful, unburdened by any obligation, inner or outer, to get stiff on command; performance yields to uncalculated, loving sexual communion, aimed not toward ecstasy, but *already* expressive of ecstasy.

A partial approach to "sexual" problems, be it that of a sex therapist, a psychiatrist, a Freudian or Jungian analyst, a "New Age" channeler, a "religious" counsellor, a bodywork specialist, or anyone else who espouses a particular system, is bound to fail, simply because it does not take into account the totality of who it is "treating." Eclecticism doesn't necessarily work either, nor does a synthesis of different systems. What does work is what happens when therapists or counsellors are deeply enough centered in their own being to *be unbound* to any particular system; they may draw from different systems, but they don't dilute or compromise their integrity in order to do so. They teach only what they *intimately* know. They do not follow a set program, but rather permit the dynamics of their encounter with their client to determine the direction of the session, making as much room as possible for the spontaneous, moment-to-moment expression of Truth, however paradoxical it might *appear...*

Masturbation is sex bereft of awakened love, sex gone to mind, sex burdened by the obligation to make us feel better. Masturbation is a marriage of genitals and mind, orchestrated by a deeply wounded psyche, a long-time suppression of being. In its marriage, love is but an ideal, or a romanticized parody of itself. Its wedding vow is to come on command. Its children are enervation, depression, and delusion. Its hobbies are interior decorating, acting, and watching television, especially stimulating shows. And, all the while, it secretly weeps for its transformation. Do not turn from its sobs. Do not fuck them away. They are *your* tears...

19

Into The Heart
Of Rejuvenative Orgasm

Orgasm is not necessarily equivalent to ecstasy. Usually, it is no more than the peak of pleasure, the climax of genital frenzy, the hungrily anticipated dissolution of erotic build-up, the pseudo-rapturous rupturing of copulatory tension, all of which have far, far more to do with the manipulative maximizing of sexual sensation than with real sexual intimacy, with its fluidly spontaneous, already-happy, already-unstressed interplay of love, subtlety, pure feeling, and open-eyed wildness.

When orgasm follows sex that was engaged in for the purpose of making one feel better, then it is, at best, but pleasurable release, however intense it might be. It is *not* ecstasy. How can it be, when its prelude is so emotionally diseased, so full of unexamined automaticities, so busily deluded, so easily invaded by fantasy, so, so desperate to feel better? Orgasm is ecstatic when sex is ecstatic, and sex is only truly ecstatic when we come to it already loose and happy, already open, already unpressured, already unburdened by any craving to have something special occur.

Come to sex already clean, already free of distress, already naturally relaxed, already full of love and passion, already uninhibitedly open to feeling the full range of our feelings, as well as our partner's, and then ecstasy is already the case — that is, ecstasy is established as the *foundation*, not the goal, and therefore orgasm is free of expectations that it produce ecstasy. In fact, orgasm in such a situation is not expected to do anything in particular. When it happens, it is not at all discontinuous with what preceded it, but rather is a glorious intensification of full-bodied joy, an overwhelmingly blissful explosion throughout our entire being, streaming and rushing with delicious force in all directions at first, then pouring and rushing up and up, up through our heart (occasionally even beginning there), flooding our skull, rising and rising, pulsating out and out, enveloping and expanding our body, leaving us wonderfully and unmistakably rejuvenated, feeling even closer to our lover than before...

Typical orgasm, however sweet it might feel, however intense its waves or spasms, does not rejuvenate, but drains, especially in men. Orgasm for men is all too often no more than a discharge of excess energy, an ejaculation of tension, a contracted spasm, followed by enervation, dullness, emotional oblivion, relief, drowsiness, and sleep, as though orgasm were but a kind of sleeping pill. Orgasm cannot enliven the heart if love is not present, nor can it fill the whole body if there is holding, physical or emotional, anywhere in one. Even at the moment of ejaculation, most men control themselves, repressing their vulnerability, emptying themselves of their desire, no longer pumping any energy into a display of intimacy, drifting off into sleep, not realizing that they have been asleep all along. Thus do men tend to fuck away their passion, their contraction of being, especially of torso, forcing the energy of orgasm to dissipate itself in the limbs and pelvis, thereby sedating the whole system.

Typical orgasm drains women in a different way; its soporific or de-stressing effect may still be present, but is usually not as strong as an underlying dissatisfaction, a suddenly naked sense of emotional and spiritual loneliness, which may lead to a craving for more sex (and thus more distraction from loneliness and emotional isolation), or for some real intimacy. The pleasure and relief of orgasm may mask this, but not for long. Some women don't expose their dissatisfaction because they don't want to hurt their partner, or make him even more self-conscious about doing it right; they'd rather go on suffering, inwardly complaining, all the while hurting their partner even more with their martyred silence. Other women speak of their dissatisfaction, sometimes blaming their partner, and more often blaming themselves, thereby creating more and more tension, and thus an increasingly desperate urge for release, particularly through genital manipulation. Some women go further, seeking therapy, other lovers, new circumstances, perhaps even a "spiritual" life. Few, however, really wake up to what they are doing, truly understanding that the distance they so often feel after sex was there *all along*, obscured by fantasy and hyped sensation.

Women who have awakened to the point of being essence-centered do not look for happiness, but are already happy; they do not hope to be fulfilled through sex, but rather celebrate their fullness and womanliness through sex, craving nothing, not even multiple orgasms, for they are *already* orgasmic, in or out of sex. Their orgasms are so complete, so deeply rejuvenating, so thrillingly expansive, so open to the currents of Eternity, so deep and so wide, so lush with song and vibrant silence, that they do not crave more. Theirs is the orgasm of unqualified surrender, the ecstasy and nectared swoon of multi-dimensional flowering, petalling out and out...

Men, in general, are less disturbed by the distance that follows (and accompanies and precedes) sex, except when it is paved with distaste, guilt, or a strong urge to escape. Many men are not even aware of such distance; they are, from long practice, all but numbed to their feeling dimension. Other men, more sensitive, notice their lack of intimacy with their partner, but feel powerless to do much more about it than try to think or therapize it away — they, having distanced themselves from their raw male power in their embracing of sensitivity, have but fled their balls, finding refuge in helplessness, which they mistakenly associate with vulnerability. They are as obsessed with being soft as their more macho counterparts are with being hard. Some men blame their partner, some blame their past, some blame their penis, some pretend everything's just fine, some can't do it without a jugful of wine, some don't want to look, some insist on doing it by the book, and almost all are looking for solace, for relief, for immunity, wanting to "fix" their sexual problematicness without exploring the roots of it.

Few men have the guts to get to the heart of the matter, to take the journey of being that necessitates letting go of control and stepping into the Unknown, not the unknown of post-coital oblivion or of sleep, but the unknown that is populated by one's depths, the unknown that pulsates not only with archetypes of behaviour and mind-free feeling, but also with Eternal Unknowableness, the endless Mystery of Being Itself. This is not a metaphysical journey, nor is it merely a hero's journey — it is a passage into the full embodiment of living Truth, asking everything of one. A man, to make this passage, cannot just rely on sensitivity, nor on power, nor on love alone; all of it, all of him, must work together, no matter what the weather, so that he might become a vulnerable warrior, overflowing with both exquisitely subtle sensitivity and exultantly muscular force, simultaneously strong and soft, potent and yielding, alive and present in his every thrust, unafraid of Woman, free to love her with nothing withheld.

The orgasms of such men are deeply ecstatic and sweetly rejuvenating, fully surrendered celebrations of sexual love, pure offerings rocketing all afire into the welcoming flowering of awakened Woman. Such men die to themselves not only during orgasm, but also during sex. They neither perform, nor deliberately try to please, nor fantasize, nor hold back, nor lose touch with their partner, nor act, nor react, nor break contact at orgasm. They only love, not fearing their forcefulness, nor their tenderness...

When we make orgasm the goal, we only screw ourselves.

There is no point in trying to "have" better orgasms, if the rest of our life is not open to something deeper than mere rearrangement. Real orgasm is ecstasy. It cannot be produced by technique, nor by hope, nor by mind-fucking. It requires a balanced, passionate life that doesn't cling to safety, but that is willing to again and again rock the boat, to make habit-upsetting waves. A mediocre or deluded life cannot include ecstatic orgasm, anymore than it can suddenly become awakened and spirit-true at physical death.

The *totality* of our life must be taken into account when orgasm is being "worked on." Otherwise, orgasm is just one more consolation, one more obstruction to a sane life, one more way of wasting energy, one more way of postponing the leap we must, sooner or later, take. To restore orgasm to its rejuvenative, ecstatic function, we must be passionately committed to the awakening process, not just now and then, but *continuously*, so that we eventually develop a true center of being, a center that cannot be lost even in the wildest yielding of sex, a center that expands infinitely during orgasm, motivelessly embracing one and all...

20

When Homosexuality's Knot
Is Undone

Homosexuality is, for almost all who participate in it, no more than an avoidance of real intimacy, a fear-fueled obsession with erotic stimulation (mostly in men), wraparound security (mostly in women), and pleasurably consoling distraction. But then so too is almost all heterosexuality — it's the same old tale of sex being used as an outlet for stress, a manufacturer of romantic delusion, a reinforcer of egoistic habit, and a psychological garburetor, all of which are but confessions of having burdened sex with the obligation to make us feel better. The real issue here is the abuse of sex, not the morality of particular sexual practices. Homosexuality, in its diseased form, is only one more symptom of the suppression of being, albeit one of the most revealing symptoms, for its controversy and still-widespread condemnation spotlight it, especially in contrast to so-called normalcy.

Suppression of being (which is synonymous with fragmentation of self, and with absence of center) is the root cause of all neurosis, homosexual and otherwise. What I want to discuss here are the secondary causes of homosexuality, those influences that arise from the turning away from the totality of oneself; such influences do not always create overt homosexuality, but they are fertile soil for it.

Let us begin with male homosexuals, and ask why so many of them behave like parodies of women. Why do they adopt such exaggeratedly "feminine" gestures? Why the overly theatrical tone, the puppet-like simpering and excessive bouncing-about, the highly stylized flaunting and suggestiveness, the often grotesquely advertised availability? Just for whom are these peacocks spreading their fans?

For Daddy, or, more precisely, for a suitable stand-in for Daddy.

The point is to attract Daddy's attention, to simultaneously turn him on and keep him at a distance, welcoming little more than his hoped-for hardness, his almost anonymous thrust and withdrawal, his aesthetically shadowed face, his loveless embrace, mistaking his engorged presence for real attention. Thus does a deeper longing get fucked away — a piece of ass, a hard cock or two, an exchange of fluids and little else, a few rushes and a cramped release, perhaps some guilt to get the next rush up on its feet, perhaps some cleanup, some rearranging of face and fantasy, some straightening of clothes and roles, and it isn't all that different than most heterosexual encounters, is it? Two bodies rubbing together, making a fire that's all heat and no light, pretending that everything's all right, or that *this* is the way it has to be, desperately trying to fuck away their misery...

So "Daddy" takes the bait, and fucks "Mommy." One man, usually the more outwardly feminine, plays "Mommy," and the other man gets to fuck "her" without having to get close to an actual woman — he acts out getting close, at least physically, without having to *directly feel* his mother through the body of another woman. Getting to fuck "Mommy" is not a love-act, but an act of violence, of power-lust, of being in charge in a way that was not possible as a child, except in fantasy. Getting to fuck "Mommy" is about revenge, or compensation, for being dominated, for being so profoundly helpless before and dependent upon his mother for so many years. Neurotic dominance, or power without love, may or may not have been the case, but helplessness and utter dependence were once realities for him. To the point: if that primal dependency was mishandled by his mother, made a problem of in some significant way, then he quickly learned to both crave *and* loathe dependency, repetitiously manipulating himself in later years to appearing independent, or to playing out exaggerated dependency-games to attract mothering, or at least a facsimile of mothering.

Such a male made, and is making, an unnecessary association between dependence and entrapment, and also between vulnerability and helplessness. Whether he twists himself to attract mothering, or to flee it, he is self-bound to "Mommy" — she, or the spectre of her, haunts him most of the time, subtly dictating his direction, ever cutting the channels for his excitation. There is no escape for him, not even in promiscuity. He can surround himself with men, but she is there, especially in mind. He cannot completely abandon her, for she, the real she, is universal. She, beyond the personal, is the sustaining Power of all that is, the Eternal Womb out of which all emerge and return. Everyone, however slightly, intuits this, but few make it important.

The male homosexual who is driven to fuck "Mommy" over and over again, craves connection, real connection, but flees or sabotages it, just as his father did. With desperate, endarkened need, he sucks at a surrogate nipple, or erection, taking in artificial milk, finding what pleasure he can in his oral ritual, trying to maximize his sensory thrill, even as something hidden in him longs for ecstasy, for love, for real communion...

And what of the man who plays "Mommy," the man who craves feeling "her" being penetrated, or sexually overwhelmed? His strategy as a child was probably to empathize with his mother, especially if she was neurotically passive. Such a mother could easily inundate her son with herself, *enlarging* herself through his absorption of her, thus exploiting his turning to her for refuge or relief from his father. Or the man who plays "Mommy" may have been so actively dominated by his mother, so completely overpowered and emotionally invaded, that he learned submission as a survival tactic. As an adult, he, to get "Mommy" out of his system (however briefly), invites in a strong, penetrating force, a surrogate either of "Daddy" or of the kind of man his mother secretly desired (and wanted *him* to be).

As such, male homosexuality is but a dramatization of unresolved power struggles, enacted through sexual channels. Either fuck "Mommy" or be her getting fucked. In both cases, "Mommy" is dominated, "manhandled," temporarily deflated, and definitely degraded. Revenge, however, is only part of this; deep, desperately concealed need is also present, revealed in the nervous intensity and debonair despair that characterizes so much of male homosexuality. Such need is but the need for real mothering, for truly loving nurturance, a need that unfortunately rarely shows itself in its fullness, usually appearing only as neediness, or need that is polluted by mental manipulativeness...

Neediness *sucks;* real need gives through its very nakedness of asking. Neediness is indirect; real need is direct. Neediness complains; real need expresses. Neediness crawls; real need has dignity, the dignity that comes from standing one's true ground. Neediness is a disease of feeling — the heartfelt confession of real need is the cure. We all need mothering. There is no escape from this, no alternative, no flight away from it, gross or subtle, no immunity from it, none!

Embodying a fuckable caricature of womanhood/mothering, or attacking it through genital aggression and emotional recoil, only distances the male homosexual (*and* everyone else in a similar position) from making good use of the maternal or feminine. And what would that good use be? It is developing the capacity to lovingly and sanely mother oneself to such an extent that one can both recognize and let in authentic mothering from other sources, human and otherwise, without any diminishment of being. Our bond with our mother, whatever her degree of irresponsibility might have been with us, is ours to turn into bondage, or ours to use to deepen our resonance with what we ultimately and presently depend upon for our very life.

Male homosexuality ordinarily only involves "Daddy" as a prop, a buttoned-up or roughhouse collection of paternal traits attached to an inflatable cock. In general, "Daddy" is weak compared to "Mommy," even if he beats her, or thoroughly dominates her. He is little more than personified thrust, big or small. His appearance is secondary — for all too many men, their father was (and is) a vague figure, large but transient, dense but ephemeral, wandering about somewhere behind the promise of "Mommy's" nourishment, wandering in and out of war and work, his paycheck in one hand, his despair in the other, his stride not his, his boyhood crushed far behind his mind-ridden eyes. Sometimes he stumbled into the foreground, perhaps even setting up camp there, delivering punishment and even terror, but "Mommy" remained the refuge, the womb, the harbour. She might have been a stagnant or even toxic harbour, but she was (and for many, still is) a harbour, a fecund promise, a mirage of safety, potent with lullabies, persisting long after "Daddy" has had his say.

There is an instinctive understanding women have of mothering that men can never truly have, a maternal knowingness that can be obscured, but never obliterated. Men who have no center of being are terrified of mothering-energy, terrified of being consumed or sucked into nothingness, terrified of emotional surrender, terrified of ecstasy, terrified of real vulnerability, the kind of vulnerability that is a source of strength. Such men are afraid to fully embody and express their need for love, intimacy, and Truth, because doing so requires that they break through their entrapping assumptions about themselves, not just mentally, but on all levels. Getting thus to the heart of the matter takes guts — it cannot be done if one is fucking away one's gut-level feelings, or hanging out in highrises of mind, calculating one's every move, nor can it be done if awakening is not made a priority senior to all other priorities.

If after becoming stably centered in his core of being, a man still leans toward homosexuality, then it is natural for him. However, almost all male homosexuality would disappear, at least in its genital fixation, if

true center was established in men, just as would masturbation, pornographic fascination, neurotic heterosexuality, and the use of fantasy
during sex. With center, with integrity, with harmony of body, mind,
and spirit, the natural is more than enough for us. What would be left
of male homosexuality then would be a few rare cases of real sexual
lovers, and, more importantly, an ease of intimacy between men, a
camaraderie both sensitive and strong, a kinship both tender and
refreshingly rough. Such men would not fear women, but love them,
with a passion both subtle and muscular, a passion bright with force,
fluidly moving between giving and receiving, offering not only the
fullness of their manhood, but the fullness of their surrender to the
forces governing Life. Such is spirit incarnate in its manly aspect,
luminous with initiatory force and fearless receptivity. Such is the joy of
being a man. It is he who dissolves, awakens, and stands true in God,
not the effeminate male, nor the hardened male. It is he who loves. It is
he who leaps for joy, full of shining boy. It is he who embraces
Woman...

Let us now consider female homosexuality. Why is it so much more
sisterly than male homosexuality is brotherly? Simply because it is
earthier, warmer, less genitally-obsessed, less erotically-exploitive, less
concerned with escape — it is far more communal, far more tribal,
much richer in myth. Female homosexuality is closely linked to feminist and post-feminist philosophy and metaphor, whereas male sexuality can claim no such corresponding link of equivalent breadth and
historical implication. In the past twenty years, there have been an
abundance of books, seminars, and "growth" workshops just for
women, many of them drawing no firm line between homosexual and
non-homosexual women. Sisterhood has been the dominant cry, however strident, however self-enclosing, however cultic at times, a cry that
has permeated our culture, a compelling call to band together, to bond
level upon level, to deepen ancient and present ties, to work, celebrate,
and harvest a common ground.

Men, by comparison, are offered no such call, except for the faint
whisper of occasional men's gatherings (with their tendency toward
impotent bravado, ballyhooed vulnerability, and incessant sensitivity),
so that their brotherhood exists mainly in the degraded form of pub get-
togethers, stag parties, moments of sport, square-shouldered discus-
sions, and military comingling, almost all of it cut off from real
intimacy. "Gay" gatherings of men exist in isolation from other men;
the male homosexual is an outcast from his fellow men, an ostracized

brother, a faggot, a disgrace to manhood. On the other hand, the female homosexual is not ordinarily an outcast, but rather an adventuress, at least in the eyes of many heterosexual women. Sisterhood runs deep; brotherhood, without war, runs dry. Sisterhood does not fear vulnerability, tenderness, and affection; brotherhood all too often does.

Again and again, brotherly love dies impaled on the twin spikes of invulnerability and cowardice, silently screaming for real compassion from men, rather than a barrage of shoulds and shouldn'ts. Or brotherly love twists itself into unillumined homosexuality, compensating for its impotence with exaggerations of style and role. Sisterly love is much closer to true intimacy; at worst, it is but avoidance of men, an obsessive shunning of male force, but more often than not, it is a coming together, a friendliness, an ease that may frown upon, but does not usually condemn, female homosexuality.

Look at the workshop and literary offerings for women — celebrations of the feminine, reconnections with "Goddess" energies, "empowerment" rituals both modern and ancient, psychological alchemy, more and more life-giving definitions of what it is to be a woman, and on and on, penetrating the mainstream of our culture, gradually establishing a bridge for women with their collective past. This bridge is not so much with the traditional, or male version, of history, but is with womanhood's psychospiritual history, their most fertile myths of being, their inner stories, their archetypal female energy and potential. Certainly, much of this is giddy with itself, far too self-congratulatory, plugged up with feminist ideology, but more than enough of it hits home, breathing life into modern women, especially those who are living unconventional lives.

Homosexual women are thus less estranged from other women than are their male counterparts from non-homosexual men. They are, in however twisted a manner, affirming their womanhood, surrounding themselves with it, letting themselves be flooded and supported by the maternal, whereas homosexual men are, in general, not so much engaging with and celebrating their manhood, as they are reacting against the maternal and their deep need for it in female form. Men often associate homosexuality with weakness, femininity, submissiveness, and other signs of "unmanliness," while women are more inclined to associate homosexuality with refuge, however neurotic it might be, a perhaps even admirable refuge from men, an intensification of strength through numbers, to offset the loveless aggression of most men.

Female homosexuals tend to cling to the maternal, encircling it with the very hardness they so readily decry in men. They overprotect their softness, denying it sufficient contact with male force, fearing rape (gross or subtle); thus does their softness, their capacity for deep welcome, slowly atrophy and dry up, for lack of contact not with typical male force, but with the sensitive yet very potent force of a truly centered man, he who abides in the native integrity of his being. Such men are undeniably rare, but they do exist — if the door is shut to all men, then even such a man cannot come in.

The true male, the vulnerable warrior, the one whose awakening is full-bodied and coexistent with raw passion, stands in a no-man's-land, ignored or misunderstood by almost all of his fellows, homosexual or not, and feared by all those women who are in recoil against male power and passion. The true male's hardness, though extremely potent, is not a weapon, nor an ego-bearer, nor an avoidance of softness; rather, it is a celebration both of thrust and of surrender to the feminine, just as vulnerable as it is muscular, just as direct as it is multi-dimensional, springing forth not from desperation, nor from revenge, nor from a craving to prove something, but from joy, ballsy, juicy joy, empathetic joy, the kind of joy that soars with the coming together of male and female...

Now back to female homosexuality. If after becoming truly centered, a woman still leans to homosexuality, then it is natural for her. The establishment of such center would, however, result in the disappearance of almost all female homosexuality, leaving in its place a deep, non-genital intimacy between women, a sisterliness so rich and so loving that it could whole-heartedly welcome men in, not just wimpy, "sensitive" men who spout feminist jargon, but true men. Such women would not fear these men, but would *love* them, receiving them with a passion both uninhibited and discriminating. Such women would demand the best of each other, and of men, their demand being less of a push, and more of an invitation. They would mother without smothering, their own intuition being their authority, their fertility of being not a bargaining tool, nor a kind of seduction, but rather a place of birthing, both for themselves, and for men.

Such women would live in communion with the Source of All, letting themselves more and more fully incorporate Its Intent and Love. They would not snipe from feminist pulpits, but would speak from their depths, allowing their natural voice to bloom. They would give without giving themselves away. They would know ecstasy. They would not be ladies, but women. They would remain capable of melting with sexual bliss, pooling out and out, drawing together ocean and river, petalling out and out, softly exploding, meeting their lover in a light both lusty and sublime, again and again welcoming his fire, his fluid, sinewy desire, his need, his dying, his crying, his exultation, his birthing, his power, his full worth. The true woman lives free of hope. She no longer clings to seduction, despair, reactive sorrow, misaligned anger, self-pity, passivity, or neurotic activity — she has gone past mediocrity, past obsession with security, past ideology, past the deification of independence, past being right, into the heart of now, the eternal fecundity of now, the grief and laughter and love and pain and joy of now, the undiluted feeling of now, her participation so full that she is in simultaneous harmony with the temporal and the Timeless, bright with relational joy, ever honouring her need for deep intimacy...

Homosexuality, in almost all cases, does not fulfill such need (and nor does heterosexuality, bisexuality, or asexuality) because it all too often is used to make us "feel better," via stress-release, pleasurable distraction, and egoic consolation. It is ordinarily a confession of pain, of separation, of alienation — it can be a platform for righteousness, or it can be a stage, a place of transition, *not* into conventional heterosexuality, but into real sex, sex in which ecstasy is not the goal, but rather the foundation, sex that is a celebration of being, rather than a compensation for suppression of being. Homosexuality clarifies male and female roles in our culture through its exaggeration of them. Let us learn from such spotlighting, rather than blinding ourselves attacking *or* defending homosexual practices. Let us free our sexuality from the obligation to make us feel better. Let us make room in ourselves for the true man and the true woman, letting their meeting inflame our awakening impulse, letting their greeting rejuvenate us, letting their love-cries undo our deepest disguise, letting their interplay ever enrich and expand us...

21

Masochism And Sadism

Masochism and sadism are but symptoms of the dissociation of power from love — they have in common a deep collapse of heart that leaves the capacity both for giving and for receiving force marooned from empathetic sensitivity. Doing-power that ought to have been flooding upward from the belly to the heart either bypasses the chest (leaving it sunken, defeated, or rigidly inflated), invading the neck and head (and arms), seeking expression through mental activity, or it marches down to the genitals and perineal region (and legs), looking for release through sexual discharge. Thus does energy intended for a belly-to-chest, or power-to-love interchange and communion gather in the thinking mind and the genital area, creating a link between the two that is utterly uninformed by any heartfelt sensibility.

Masochism prostrates itself on this link, this hotline highway, moaning for impact, while sadism sits behind the wheel of every steamroller hurtling up and down the pavement, both its feet pressuring the accelerator. However, masochism is no simple highway kill, but rather a strategy, almost always unconscious, to seek liberation, or self-dissolution, through getting flattened, crushed, mutilated, or otherwise violated, a strategy whose very failure to fully realize its goal only goads it on, inviting and creating bigger and bigger steamrollers. Even murder isn't fulfilling enough — the plug gets pulled out, but the drama, or program, still exists in subtle form, merely awaiting physical embodiment once again...

And sadism too knows no thoroughly fulfilling release. No matter how stimulating its exercise, no matter how rich its revenge, no matter how erotic its violence, it is a stranger to ecstasy, an outcast from the very love it seeks through its rituals, a frustrated child writhing in loveless catharsis, its room a motherless womb, its windows black, its eventual exhaustion of its drivenness again and again teaching it to associate release, however partial, with blindly destructive force. It is but a perversion of the masculine, just as masochism is a perversion of the feminine.

Masochism takes what sadism gives, without any real protest, getting as much dark thrill and grovelling glory as possible from the encounter, reinforcing and validating its identity through the presence of its bruises, inner and outer. Curling in on itself, masochism lets itself be driven or beaten to the point of amorphousness, of raw fleshiness, until it exists in a seemingly boneless condition, catatonically infantile, or even grotesquely foetal, quiveringly naked and spineless, like a snail torn from its shell, and, at the same time, it yearns to explode, to expand, to die, to be *completely* released through what it draws to itself. Masochism is but contraction of being, a state of gross passivity, wallowing in self-degradation, luxuriating in its lowliness, playing small to attract what's big, or seemingly capable of beating it into transcendence of itself.

Of course, such transcendence doesn't happen, because masochism is far too busy with its script, far too bound up in its abjectness, to be truly permeable to love, sanity, and God-communion. It is far too committed to acting like a victim. Masochism craves being fucked into oblivion, or a state of extreme undifferentiation, but it only gets fucked numb and dumb. It may want to be split asunder by an enormous cock, or by a blackleather-jacket gang-bang, or by a deliciously painful whipping, physical or verbal, but it only gets fucked senseless, fucked into a dead peace, its desired rupturing of self only a rupturing of blood vessels, or a vicious crushing of vulnerability. And let us not forget guilt: masochism plays the side that gets to "do it," while sadism plays the side that gets to wield the parental whip.

Sadism is obsessed with penetration, especially sexual, endlessly polishing and upgrading its thrust, ever honing its lust, seeking suitable softnesses it can invade, especially seductively resistive softnesses. Sadism is a rapist. It is loveless force, compulsively hard, using fucking as a weapon. Twisted power, or cage-ripened rage, does the fucking, assisted by a corresponding aberration of mind, or if there isn't any fucking, twisted power travels to the mind (and vice versa), calculatingly raping the environment, clearcutting its forests, shitting in its rivers, getting insanely logical, erecting row upon row of architectural monstrosities, fluorescent-lit caskets of dehumanized structure whose sharp-edged invulnerability is personified in the modern superhero, the man of steel (although he has, in the past two decades, become slightly more human, reflecting our culture's ever so slight shift to a more female perspective). And does not the super-hero yearn to fall apart, to let go his iron grip? Does he not tire of his exploits? Yes, but not enough. The superhero must weep, weep himself beyond merely reactive sorrow into pure, unrestrained grief for his loss of love and integrity, until his grief is continuous with a sobering joy...

Sadism is the belly-steeled cock gone to mind, propagandizing the whole body with fascist intent, glistening like a nuclear warhead, its tip wet with pearly poison, its balls squeezed tight by its contraction of being. On and on it goes, desperately doing its best to obliterate every appearance of the maternal. However, there is no real escape from the maternal, no lasting immunity from its presence, not even in the most antiseptic abstractions of sadistic impulse.

Sado-masochism is but a refusal to love. It is an abuse of doing-power, a stalemated parent-child conflict projected onto the entire world, a cul-de-sac of diseased feeling. Go find its hidden need, go not to end its impulse, but to untwist it, to unravel its neurotic mind-connections, to illuminate its roots. Go to its heart, go straight to the broken one inside it, the one whose tiny fists have been hammering for so long against the inside of your chest, the one who has wept for so long for your unrestrained embrace. Breathe wide the walls, breathe open the windows, cry and laugh the ceiling into pure sky, invite spirit in, and mind-free power, and love, and joy, and wise wonder...

22

Ecstasy Is Not Elsewhere

We cannot produce ecstasy, nor can we stimulate ourselves into it —
there is *no* copulatory ritual that will transport us into ecstasy's realm,
however pleasurable its sensations might be. The very peak of sexual
stimulation, if reached without too much numbing, positions us for the
release we've been craving, the climax of excitation, the thrilling
discharge of all the tension we've built up through our genital exercise.
Orgasm, the promised payoff, the eruption of the peak, the big moment,
the little death, the all-too brief break from the mind's chatter —
whatever we might associate with it, orgasm is not necessarily ecstasy.
If what precedes orgasm is not ecstasy, then orgasm is at best but a bolt
of pleasure, a few waves of intense thrill; even if such orgasm is a storm,
a great bursting, an intoxicating undulation of delicious current, a
swooning dissolution of boundaries, it is still not ecstasy, but only a
cul-de-sac of quickly spent excitation.

Ecstasy is an intensification of happiness, not the happiness that
depends upon something in particular happening, but the happiness
that is inherent to Being, the happiness that is *already* the case when
we are standing our true ground, no matter what our mood or circumstance. If such happiness is not present *before* we begin to engage in
sex, then our sexual act is precisely that, an *act* whose predictably-
scripted dramatics are intended to produce "good" feelings and intimacy, an act that is but fleshed-out fantasy, starring us in our search
for ecstasy.

Almost everyone of us is looking for ecstasy, not seeing, except perhaps
intellectually, that our very looking is the problem. The assumption
that ecstasy is elsewhere, at the end of a series of steps, or at the point
of maximal sexual stimulation, or there if only we "do it right," is
self-propagandizing bullshit, keeping those who are "in the know" in

business, and keeping those who insist on playing customer or consumer chained to their misery. Ecstasy exists in the heart of each moment, in the very depths that we flee in our compulsive search for pleasurable release. Ecstasy is the full-bodied feeling of unexploitable freedom, a feeling that pervades our *entire* being.

Ecstasy is not a reward, nor a product, nor is it at the end of a rainbow. It is *here.* It is the open face of real happiness, the shout of the awakened heart. It is uninhibited communion with the Source of All.

It is not afraid of fear, nor is it afraid of pain. It is our very nature, the passion of our deepest purity, the celebration of undiluted love.

When we do not rest in our being, when we are asleep to our true condition, then we are cut off from ecstasy. As a counter-effort to our self-imposed isolation, we busy ourselves creating surrogates of ecstasy and various routes to these, be they hedonistic, ascetical, religious, pornographic, drug-based, or whatever. With glib stubbornness, we erode ourselves in our repetitious obsession with these paths, madly believing in them, condemning or pitying those who don't salute our flag, again and again creating systems that promise to deliver the goods, to produce ecstasy, if only we faithfully follow the directions on the package — if we don't get the goods, if we remain miserable, if we don't "get it," then we are told it is because we didn't do it right or fully enough, and so we chant harder, pray more, buy yet another sex manual, work harder, go to more "growth" seminars, tighten up our belief system, get more devotional, or just give up, settling for sedation and cynicism.

Just about all of us are looking for ecstasy, not realizing that what we are looking for is ourselves, not the us that is found through simplistic emotional conversion and mental restructuring, but the us that lives outside *all* systems and *all* meaning, the us that is eternally inviolable. Looking for ourselves doesn't work, unless we look *inside* our looking. Only then can sanity emerge. Only then can love breathe us true. Only then can we make room for our woundedness and our glory.

Sex is *not* a means to ecstasy. Sex, when healthy, is an expression of already-embodied ecstasy, a total participation in intimacy not only with our partner(s), but also with the Source, a dance of both individuality and deep surrender, a fluid, spontaneous interplay of form and formlessness. Sexual ecstasy is mindless creativity, motivelessly intelligent, juicily alive and intuitive, in deep harmony with the creative force of the Source.

Ecstasy is not addictive. Only when we have turned away from ecstasy do we get addictive, simply because we then create dependency-relationships with whatever promises to deliver to us some convincing semblance of ecstasy. Our entire culture craves ecstasy, but has made a taboo against authentic ecstasy; in fact, it *is* a taboo against such ecstasy, because the ecstatic human cannot be forced to fit in, to settle for the mediocrity of a mechanical life — he or she cannot be manipulated into anything that is less than life-giving.

And so we have the seeming paradox of a society that longs for something it has forbade. This is the human dilemma, but it is a dilemma only to the sleeping. Those who have begun to awaken, even if only slightly, know that there is no hope of changing the "system" from within, and that there is no hope of awakening those who are *convinced* they aren't sleeping. This, however, is *not* apathy, nor is it a turning away, but rather a necessary acknowledgment that permits further awakening. It is vision unpolluted by hope, vision potent with healing. It is disillusionment free of bitterness and resignation, a disillusionment brimming with *sobering* joy and an unmistakable integrity of being.

Those in whom awakening has stabilized stand outside the trap everyone else is in, inviting them out, not so much with their words, but with their very presence. Some go back into the trap, planting seeds, their every step and every gesture a potent hint, their ecstasy undercover; they know the risk of what they are doing, for they, with very few exceptions, are not totally immune to our culture's mass frenzy of ecstasy-searching, distress, pseudo-love, and multidimensional addiction. It is all too easy to slip back into the dream, to play saint or teacher, to, in effect, only replace the dream of our culture with a more consoling or "spiritual" dream into which seekers can be invited, for the right price.

Ecstasy is not a dream, nor is it the pinnacle of a saintly scheme. Ecstasy is the winging of love. Ecstasy is the foundation of the truly human. It is the unqualified fullness of *now*, the exultation of being at Home, the ever-virgin embracing of *this*, now and now. Do you not recognize ecstasy? Do you not feel it streaming through you, and *as* you, however quietly, however subtly? Do you not long for it?

Adapt to ecstasy, instead of to its substitutes, knowing that your destiny is to embody it. *Now.*

23

Pornography's Engorged Empire

Pornography is the machinery of eroticism, designed to catalyze and intensify sexual excitation in a context devoid of real intimacy and love; it is a businesslike response to the craving of those who have turned away from ecstasy to be pleasurably compensated for their trouble. Pornography is not just limited to centerfolds, stroke-magazines, "adult" movies, sado-masochism photos, advertising, and romance novels, but is the style, or strategy, of those who employ fantasy in their sex life, especially as a means of "getting turned on" or staying aroused — they bind their sexuality to their minds, deifying juicy stimulation, reducing their partner to a more or less enticing prop in their masturbatory drama, not seeing that they are only fucking themselves, not realizing that they have only enslaved themselves to the repetition of loveless genital release. To truly enjoy sex is impossible for them, for they do not enter its domain nakedly present, but come in already addicted to preconceived erotic expectation and ritual, already stranded from spontaneity, joy, and integrity...

Pornography's fire does not purify, but only inflames and engorges, both distracting us from our doubt, anxiety, and distress, and also bloating us with such heated urge that we seemingly have to have some sort of relief, or discharge of energy. However, such release does not rejuvenate or liberate us, but only dulls us, leaving us less motivated than ever to getting to the heart of what is troubling us, of what is driving us to so desperately seek the sedation of masturbatory release.

Pornography's promise of satisfaction and release is fundamentally no different than that of religion — both exploit and market human alienation and separateness (from authenticity, love, and God), both are fueled by hope, guilt, desperation, and mistaken identity, both are escapes from what must be directly faced, and both are institutionalized (societal or personal) perversions of deep human longing. Heaven, Christian and otherwise, is but pornography of spirit — it is the unilluminated mind's romanticized version of the sacred, teeming with hope's phantoms, crammed with egocentric satiation, its sky blackened by winged hypocrisy and cherubic oblivion, its streets lined with horny celibates, instant saints, and greedy slaves, all of whom mechanically proclaim their allegiance to their parental abstraction of God, propagandizing themselves ever further into their surrogate of the Real. Do you not see spiritual seekers bowing before their airbrushed blowup of God, rubbing themselves into a state of swollen tension, their minds jammed with tomorrow, their hearts clogged with reactive sorrow, ever submitting to a suppression of being that only *amplifies* the need for some sort of consoling release? Do you not see the charade, all the egos in holy robes referring to themselves as souls? Do you not see how prayer and meditation have all but been reduced to remedies, serving the very same gratifications as pornography?

Romance is also pornography, however unpornographic it might appear. When sexual anticipation or excitation, already fantasy-polluted, passes through the emotional center, romance occurs — it is literally a chestful of lust, radiating in all directions, packed with swooning thoughts and deliciously stimulating imagery, not to mention runaway hope, a hope enthused about union, true love, and soul-mate possibility, a hope nourished and sustained by the dissolution of boundaries between the so-called lovers, a dissolution that is far more about *collapse* than expansion. As the hyped passion fades, thoughts of betrayal and doubt creep in, however subtly at first, and the lovers eventually wonder where they went wrong, not seeing that such a sense of potential betrayal and rejection has been with them all along, obscured by the heat of their embrace, the force of their hope, and their commitment to wearing a false face. They were but fucking under artificial light, without integrity and without intelligence, blindly merging at the level of sensation and infantile craving, abandoning their boundaries instead of expanding them. Nevertheless, even though many people realize the folly of romance, they still support it, fondly and wistfully implying that it is a lovely thing, an essential part of love, when in fact it is not love at all, but only the perfumed side of pornography, just as diseased as hard-core stuff, ever selling a pleasurably consoling dream in which sentimentalized eroticism is mistaken for love, a dream swirling with narcotic haze...

Pornography must not be banned, nor repressed. Its power, once given room to breathe itself sane, only deepens and enriches our passion, for pornography is but a perversion of our longing to ecstatically stand our true ground, to throb and stream with sensual and sexual delight, to unlock and celebrate our orgasmic potential, to fully embody our capacity for love-thrill. Pornography is but a calculating child locked in a forgotten room, too lonely to weep, compulsively busying itself with self-pleasuring, having long ago given up on ecstasy, again and again seeking the perfect replication of its most satisfying releases, surrounding itself with what does the best job.

There is no point in getting righteous about how terrible pornography is, nor is there any point in playing liberal about it — merely permitting pornography to speak and exhibit itself, out of some twisted notion of human rights, does no one any good. Yes, pornography's voice must be heard, but *not* passively. It must be given room to scream and sing and wail and moan and rage and slobber itself beyond itself. Doing so is not the action of a weak or supposedly tolerant person, but is the action of one who knows his or her own pornographic inclinations so intimately that he or she is no longer fascinated by them, nor addicted to them.

Pornography will not end until we awaken to how *we* create our distress. Until then, we will crave release from the very distress we bring to ourselves, and will repeatedly betray ourselves in both the indulgence *and* the repression of our desire for such release, drowning our integrity in misguided notions of right and wrong, notions that arise not from our being, but from our minds. Make love when you are already happy, already loose, already unstressed, and you will not need to invite in your mind, nor turn the lights out...

24

Flirting

Flirting is teasing spiked with sexual innuendo. Usually, it is no more than an utterly mechanical ritual advertising one's erotic interest in another, a self-titillating presentation of one's potential availability for sex, or, more commonly, of one's sexual potency. Much is suggested, or implied, and very little is directly stated, for directness deflates the whole process, robbing flirting of much of its ceremony and colour. To the point: If flirting is but a means of self-stimulation via sexual suggestiveness, a sleazy testing of the waters, then it ought to be deflated, or exposed, so that its participants can vulnerably face each other, rather than continue to avoid each other. However, if openness is already the case, so that the dramatics of flirting are not an avoidance of depth and integrity, but rather a sensitive, passionate play upon them, then there is no need to cut through flirtatiousness, any more than there is to remove the feathers from a mating peacock, or to halt the wonderfully ragged flight of coupling butterflies...

Such flirting does not exclude, but includes. Its purpose is not to amplify and exploit lust, but to consciously celebrate it. Healthy flirting's theatricalness is both heartfelt and mischievous, both heated and subtle, generously punctuated with humour, a humour that spontaneously includes within itself a refreshingly lucid overview of the flirting itself. This overview has nothing whatsoever to do with emotional dissociation, or with isolation of oneself in the witness position (as is frequently found in body-negative meditative practice), but is as much a part of flirting (or anything else) as is the ocean part of each wave — there is no self-division, no fragmentation of being. Instead, there is integration of self, unburdened by any notion of hierarchy among the aspects of self. Everything works together, with both awareness and passion; lust is just as welcome as sublime transpersonal experience.

Unhealthy flirting is but a symptom of self-division, of separation of heart and sexuality, of love and desire, of sensation and feeling. As well, it is a method for distracting oneself from the distress of such inner fragmentation, by means of generating a mood of erotic possibility. Thus is sex reduced to an outlet for relieving stress. Thus is sex enslaved to the task of making us feel better, of pleasurably consoling us. Typical flirting is but diseased foreplay, robotically setting up the friction that seemingly necessitates some sort of release; there's no real joy in it, only lewdly winking desperation, only giggling prurience, only unilluminated suffering, only a turning away from ecstasy...

True flirting is an unrehearsed drama of love and lust, of heat and light, of rough and tender, of give and take, a dance of grace and fire, of thrust and bend, of exultant ease and delightfully unreasonable creativity. It is intimacy stripped of all solemnity and shoulds, free of all nostalgia (for the past and for the future) and cultic coupling, completely willing to pull down romance's pants. True flirting is the face of playful desire, already happy, juicy yet relaxed, turned on but not turned tight, beaming bright...

25

Jealousy Unmasked

Jealousy, especially sexual jealousy, can be exceedingly painful, as anyone who's writhed in its straitjacketed fire knows all too well. More than most of us strive to not provide fertile soil for jealousy, but still it sprouts up everywhere, with a green not of sun-embracing reach, but of venomous force and righteous paranoia. However, jealousy is not some inherently "evil" or "negative" feeling, nor is it necessarily a problem.

What matters is what we *do* with our jealousy. Do we identify with it, and thus embody its point of view? Or do we try to rise above it, thereby denying ourselves access to our depths? Or do we condemn it, sentencing it to life imprisonment, thus walling away the very vulnerability of which our jealousy is but a twisted confession? Or do we abstract it, talking about it with forced rationality and unnatural calm, even as we wonder why our emotional life is so superficial and dull?

Or do we believe in our jealousy so strongly that we do irreparable harm to one we love? Or do we run from it, avoiding any circumstance that resembles the one that seemingly first generated our jealousy, thus committing ourselves to a life of superficiality? Or do we deny that it is actually happening, while we slowly die inside, painting good cheer on our collapse of heart? Or do we make good use of our jealousy, giving it room to breathe and rage and cry, while not submitting to its version of how things are?

Jealousy is a dramatization of being rejected, whether the rejection is real or imagined. Jealousy is the blatant exposure of unillumined possessiveness, the outraged bleat of the suddenly unmasked addict, the one who has created a dependency-relationship with someone, especially a lover or spouse, and who now resents the independence, or potential independence, that is "possessing" his or her beloved. As such, jealousy is but a neurotic reaction to loss, real or not, sometimes being hard-fisted, cruel, violent, and rabid with indignant logic, and sometimes being sunken, mushy, jammed with self-pity, crammed with boxed-in sorrow, submitting to an unnecessarily hellish tomorrow. These, the male and female extremes of jealousy, work together, sharing not only a grossness of reactivity, lovelessness, and runaway mind, but also a compulsive drive to blame, blame, and then blame some more, as if to somehow *legitimize* one's extreme contraction of being.

The core of jealousy's message is "You don't love me!" or something similar, implying colossal rejection, as of an infant by its mother. Such rejection at an infantile or childhood level may well be what is being triggered by the current situation, but it is not enough to simply know this, and to then use it as an alibi, as is all too common in many "therapeutic" environments. Yes, the conscious facing of unresolved traumas is utterly necessary if one is to become fully human, but the evidence of having actually worked through such old traumas must be seen not just in counselling sessions, but in one's *present* relationships, as demonstrated by an ability to stay open, loving, and centered even in the midst of real rejection — there may be anger and tears, and all the symptoms of jealousy, but there will not be a withdrawal of self, nor an armouring of heart, nor any escape into blame. There would be force, but not violence; there would be vulnerability, but not mushiness or sunkenness; there would be real sadness, not reactive sorrow; there would be an undeniable willingness to go right *through* jealousy's realm, rather than just a righteous positioning somewhere within it. And, most of all, there would be love, or at least the all-out commitment to making room for it, rather than a tense, loveless us rigidly waiting to see if the other, the one who has apparently rejected us, is being loving, or is going to become loving toward us...

If we will only love when we are already being loved by the other, then we are prime candidates for deep jealousy — we are then chronically on the search for signs that we are not being loved, miserably sniffing around for evidence of betrayal, reducing ourselves to neurotic sleuths, sinking into obsessive suspiciousness, again and again demanding, directly or indirectly, that the other consistently demonstrate or prove their trust-worthiness. Such demonstration, however, is rarely enough for us, for we, in our jealousy, won't trust anything except our mistrust and doubt. We *expect* betrayal, and even, in a sense, crave it, so as to, with an appalling lack of awareness, recreate infantile or childhood scenarios of unresolved rejection — unfortunately, very few of us make good use of such re-creation, unknowingly "choosing" to obey its script, rather than waking up in the midst of it, not understanding, except intellectually, that lessons must be repeated until they are fully learned.

The lesson here, at essence, is to love, or to remain *truly* open to being loving, even when we are being rejected. However, the form of such love is not meek and passive, nor is it all-accepting of rejection; it is fluid, potent, passionately alive, quite capable of clean anger, more than willing to clear the temple of money-lenders. Such love does not shrink in the face of rejection, nor does it play holy or piously stand aside, clinging to religious or metaphysical belief. It radiates forth, letting everything show, letting one's essence glow, literally creating permission for the other to break through their reactivity, distress, or guilt.

When we complain that we are not being loved, we, in our very complaining, are not being loving, but are only barricading ourselves from *fully* feeling our innermost woundedness; we are, in effect, only rejecting what is most vulnerable in us, doing to *it* what we imagine is being done to us by the one who is "making" us jealous. Real love never rejects the other (or a corresponding aspect of ourselves), but it may reject something the other is *doing*. If this doing is blindly identified with by the other, then the drama of rejection takes center stage within him or her, quickly mutating into full-fleshed jealousy.

And what is jealousy? It is the open abscess of neurotic insecurity, the endarkened revelation of separateness that's been camouflaged by pseudo-intimacy. When untouched by awareness, jealousy is a mind-polluted temper tantrum, a coupling of twisted anger and lopsided hurt up on a soapbox, righteously braying about right and wrong, making far too much noise to hear its own true song.

When penetrated by open-eyed love, jealousy eases its defences, becoming but the uninhibited expression of hurt and need, a refreshingly honest confession of possessiveness, a sharing of intense yet empathetically sensitive feeling, leaving us sobered, unmasked, and loving, bright with humour, at ease with our possessiveness, no longer struggling for either ownership or for detachment, no longer enslaved to the possibility of potential rejection, no longer afraid of jealousy...

26

A Mirage of Intimacy:
The Cult of Two

Even in the seemingly steadiest of couples, married or not, there is usually some inclination toward promiscuity (even if only mentally), neatly buttoned-up and deodorized in some unswept corner of self. Envision the loyal couple, copulating only with each other, painting decency, patriotic morality, and terminally nice considerateness over their mutual masturbatory ritual, while somewhere in their minds they fuck, flirt, depant, unskirt, or romantically associate with all sorts of people, particularly those whose presence in their fantasies is most erotically stimulating or suggestive. If the couple has pious compulsions or typical religious conditioning, they will probably inwardly beat themselves for their mental infidelity, trying extra hard to act loving toward their spouse, perhaps even praying to their parental abstraction of God for forgiveness, all the while clinging to their guilt and the degraded yet darkly pleasurable sensations it so consistently delivers.

Or the couple might be more liberal, making a virtue out of their phony tolerance for various sexual practices, stuffing themselves with self-congratulation for having, or attempting to have, what sex therapists have told them is a healthy fantasy life — spicing up the sexplay, getting the mood positioned just so, finding just the right mind-movie for getting turned on and staying turned on, getting more heated and juiced-up than would be possible just from directly meeting one's partner, since such a meeting is all too often but a failure to be intimate, a mere encounter of surfaces, ego, twisted need, and unexamined habits. The very effort to get turned on, to stir up some passion, is but a confession of being turned off, or stranded from one's depths.

A couple's struggle to stay erotically consoled is akin to pumping energy into a corpse. It is a waste of energy, an avoidance of intimacy, a pitiful charade, a self-manipulation that is used to shore up and "prove" the existence of the pseudo-intimacy that the couple is so, so desperate to believe in, the pseudo-intimacy that demonstrates to others what a "loving" couple this is. To the point: a couple cannot have a truly deep and rich sex life if the rest of their life is shallow and emotionally impoverished — all they can do is again and again recreate their illusion of intimacy through their mind-directed sexing, pretending that its sensations are real feelings, pretending that sentimentality is love, and, most of all, pretending that they aren't pretending. If the sex life of a couple is fading into unmistakable mediocrity or even non-existence, it is precisely because the rest of their life is, despite its effort to appear otherwise, doing *exactly* the same thing, dying of boredom, doubt, and obsession with security. Taking fashionable risks in the bedroom only distracts them from the truth of what is actually occurring in their life together.

On and on they go, blindly reinforcing their dulling familiarity with each other, vaguely wondering why there's no natural spark between them, sometimes getting nostalgic for their early days, busily sedating their despair, resigning themselves to their lot in life, already divorced from each other in their hearts. Instead of trying to create a spark or some semblance of passion via sexual manipulativeness and fantasy, they ought to thoroughly explore the deadness between them, the no-one's land that separates them, because it is only by passing through this zone that they will *truly* meet each other, at last clearly seeing the unspoken contracts that they have made with each other to not rock the boat. If they do not enter and penetrate this zone, or at least make a genuine effort to do so, they will have only sentenced themselves to a life of dressed-up deadness and mental bureaucracy, whether they stay together or not — separation or divorce does not solve the problem, but only relocates it in each new, unexplored coupling, each new pact to not make habit-upsetting waves, to not journey together to the heart of each other's suffering and joy. The need for life-giving risk is squashed beneath the clinging to an agreement-cemented security, oozing out in a parody of itself, as promiscuous intent and neurotic power-games; thus does sex become but a compensation for stagnation.

A couple can use sex to create a mirage of aliveness, but it is only hyped-up vitality, a byproduct of desperate friction, greened by oases of hope, populated only by phantoms of mind. Why enslave sex with the obligation to make us feel more alive, more intimate, more everything? Why butcher it so? Sex ought to be an expression of our

aliveness, a celebration of coexistent love and passion, not the pro-
ducer of it! Why use sex to comfort ourselves within our entrapping
dreams? Why abuse it so?

Imagine being already awake, already happy, already throbbing with
latent passion, and *then* making love — there is no hype and no hope in
such sex, but only the rejuvenative ecstasy of going ever deeper into
Now, feeling the pulsations of Pure Being through the entire body,
feeling the joyous embodiment of unrestrained love, the intimacy so
natural and so true, the lovers ever refreshed, ever new, loving each
other through and through, now and now, hiding nothing, giving their
all, letting their dance be permeated by Eternity's call, letting their
meeting be sacred lust, ecstatic trust, and uninhibited greeting...

The loyal husband and the loyal wife are loyal only to their self-image,
their respectable mediocrity, their daily failure of nerve, their compulsive clinging to each other; again and again, they betray their hearts,
their spirits, their awakening impulse, anaesthetizing themselves to the
Truth. They are terrified of being betrayed by each other, and so make
all kinds of agreements, mostly unspoken and unknown, that are
designed to minimize or obscure the possibility and sensations of being
betrayed. They feel chronically threatened not only by what is hidden
in the other, but by what is hidden in them; rarely do they realize just
how shallow their trust is for each other, and for their own depths.
They do not establish real trust, which requires real intimacy, but only
create agreements, contracts, and truces, tediously applauding themselves for doing so, as though resignation to such bondage was their
natural destiny!

The duller a couple's inner life, the more inclined they are to be
fascinated by possibilities of stimulation, especially erotic. Some mind-
fuck themselves into romantic or pornographic fantasy; some become
obsessively flirtatious, repetitiously advertising their availability; some
"have affairs," mistaking novelty for depth, not seeing, at least initially, that they've just found another way to screw themselves; some
fuck themselves into a craved-for stupor; some fuck themselves into
secretly-desired guilt or trouble; some fuck themselves into dead ends,
clinging to their sexual capacity like drunks clutching their bottle. And
almost all scrupulously avoid waking up to what they are actually
doing, fanatically dreaming, scheming, and scheduling their lives away,
arranging almost everything, seeking distraction and fascination, dressing
up their stagnation with superficial change and near-constant occupation, "keeping busy," mechanically associating "good" feelings or love

with exaggerated stimulation, and just as mechanically passing this on to their children, over-stimulating them, then moaning about the hyperactivity of their kids, which of course must then be tied down, buttoned-up, or drugged away....

Couples, especially those who have clung to each other for a long time, like to bleat about commitment. However, mutual entrapment is not commitment, but only cowardice. Real commitment is not bondage, but rather a deep bonding, a heartfelt grounding of relationship, a *natural* byproduct of open-eyed love and trust — it is to love as embodiment is to spirit. Real commitment is a conscious surrender to the necessity and beauty of limitation, even as it enhances one's ability to abide in and feel the Infinite. Such commitment involves no contracts — its integrity is not held in place by any act of mind, nor by any cultural or parental expectation, but is *inherent* to it. By contrast, the so-called commitment of almost all couples is but neurotic imprisonment, an ever-fashionable doing of time, a self-enclosed bubble of numbing familiarity made tolerable only by endless self-stimulation, whether genital, mental, televisional, occupational, or oral.

This bubble is sanctified by marriage, applauded by all those cosily established in a similar bind. Its nature is cultic, or rigidly exclusive; it is impermeable, except when dissatisfaction is extreme, or when wakefulness is cultivated. When the bubble's in trouble, it starts seeing double, double, double your pleasure all through its joint mind, and so further exploits its capacity for kindling up "good" feelings, which are not really feelings, but only exaggerations of sensation, especially sexual. A bubble housing a couple (or a single, or a crowd) is a lonely place, afloat on a stagnant sea, a sea whose glassy waters are scarcely astir, covered with bits of shattered sun and the debris of abandoned innocence, joy, and spirit. Within the bubble, what is magnified is not heart, but only the false start, the life-negating agreements of two lonelinesses....

The answer is not non-marriage, nor non-coupling, nor non-monogamy, but rather the utter cessation of faking intimacy, of pretending that the bubble isn't a bubble, of acting as though real depth and vulnerability is being shared. The lies must be *directly* faced, and disillusionment welcomed and embraced, used as an opportunity to deepen one's awakening. All too many couples are but two strangers looking for comfort, for lasting immunity from their own pain, doing little more than blinding themselves to their depths, wherein exists not only their suffering, their hurt, their deep grief, but also their pure passion, their joy, their ever-rejuvenating Truth, their mind-free emotion. A shallow life *cannot* coexist with a deep sex life; ecstasy in sex is not possible for those who do not know ecstasy in their "regular" life. Typical coupling shuts out ecstasy, because to permit it, a couple would have to open their relationship to the imperatives of their intertwined love, including the possibility of other lovers, other directions, and even the death, or radical transformation, of the relationship itself; whatever served or enriched their mutual aliveness, however painful its integration might be, would have to be directly encountered.

There are very few couples who will risk this; most that do take such a risk are only superficially intimate, and therefore are risking little. The real risk is for those few who are already deeply bonded — much of their bond is from taking such risk, but it cannot stop being taken, and they intuitively know this, although they sometimes wish they didn't. They can only continue, doing their best to not make a problem out of insecurity. Embracing insecurity is a necessity for them, an essential part of their foundation; if they do this with integrity and passion, eventually they will know, with every cell of their body, the *inherent* insecurity of Life, the profound inevitability of change and Death, and so will enter into an ever-deepening resonance with the Great Mystery that animates us all. The passing of everything can be taken as a tragedy, or it can be taken as an occasion for recognizing the essence of what is, with both grief and joy. Grief is not mournful contraction, but rather a heartbreaking acknowledgment and celebration of loss, a compassionate spaciousness that makes room for ecstasy, the ecstasy of being, the ecstasy of living free of all bubbles, even in the midst of the deepest commitment....

Ecstasy cannot be limited to the bedroom, nor can intimacy and love; they cannot even be confined to the couple's relationship. Bubbles exclude; love doesn't. However, inclusion does not mean throwing open the doors to everyone and everything — its welcoming must involve a sensitive discrimination, a commonsensical sorting out of what is appropriate from what is inappropriate. The clearest guide to healthy inclusion is the heartfelt intuition of the couple, rather than spiritual shoulds (and all other species of should) or ambitious hopes. Yes, the bubble must expand to such permeability that it eventually disappears, leaving only a vibrant, joyously committed relatedness in its place, but it must not be forced to expand at a rate too fast for the couple, or there will be no real grounding for their openness. As they expand, they must develop a corresponding capacity for bringing integrity to their new possibilities and opportunities. They may stay together, or they may part, or they may bring others into the very heart of their relationship, whatever is most natural for them — the right direction will make itself obvious. If they remain together, they will no longer be a couple, even if they *appear* to be. They will simply be ever more willing participants in intimate relatedness, finding through their very commitment to one another's wholeness of being an increasingly profound sense of interrelatedness with all that is...

Part III

Songs & Incantations

Remembrance

The waves return, glittering with remembered sun
Ancient songs seizing our tongues
The broken pillars standing anew
The temple rising, rising, rising
The circle shining true

The waves return, carrying the work done then
Ancient songs seizing our tongues
And we stand together again
Looking through all the slumber and pain
O Breathe us strong, breathe us sure
O Breathe us strong, breathe us pure

It is time to bring forward the gifts of old
It is time to come in from the cold
It is time to build our trust anew
Let the walls rise, naked with Eternity's View
Let the walls rise, rise from our ruins
Let the walls rise, rise, rise!
And we stand together again
Ancient songs seizing our tongues
And we can only be the Truth we must speak

Our hearts are wounded but glowing
Our power is trembling but growing
O Breathe us strong, breathe us sure
O Breathe us strong, breathe us pure
Is not the temple rising, rising, rising?
Are not our days wonder-spun?
Are we not lovers with the Undying One?

Is not the temple rising, rising, rising?
Here we are, gathered from afar
Each of us a spark from a waking star
O Flame us bright, flame us steady
O Flame us bright, flame us ready
And we stand together again
Ancient songs trembling with our name
The temple rising, rising, rising
The circle shining true

Blue Burns The Night

Coming through the gates
Coming through strong
Veins apopping, body asweat
The gates so high and so wide, the clouds piled dark and bright
Blue burns the night
Blazing is his sight

Coming through the gates
Coming through strong
His legs a bronzed blur, his heels dust-winged
The gates pulsating green, inlaid with every heart's dream
Blue burns the night
Wild is his spirit-scream

Coming through the gates
Coming through strong
Coming through clear is he, hunger passing pride
Off comes the armour, off comes the plumed headgear
Gone to nothing is the root of fear
Blue burns the night
Soul-lit is his every tear

Coming through the gates
Coming through strong
His heart streaming through his eyes, his stride ever new
His body earth and stars, his mind cloudless sky
His guide his innermost cry
Blue burns the night
Ripe is his every goodbye

Coming through the gates
Coming through strong
And through, through is he, through the gates
Through the holy doors
Through, through the secret, the secret loosed all around
The undreaming passion from toe to crown
The Great Wonder gazing through his eyes,
Enjoying Its every disguise
Explaining nothing and revealing everything
Blue burns the night
True is the light

Coming through the gates
Coming through strong
And through, through is he
Into what escapes all naming and all blaming
And through, through is he
Blue burns the night
True is the light
And I am loosed
I am, I am, I am loosed, loosed, loosed, I am loosed...

This The Open Ground

This the open ground
This the pure eagle's sound
This, this the breathing Earth
This, this the timeless dream
This, this the crystalline stream
This, this the breakthrough supreme

Take the grief from your brow
And wash the revenge from your now
Go, go where the river is dancing white
Go, go where you left your spirit-sight
Do you not feel the eagle feather in your hair?
Have you forgotten it's still there?

Fly, fly the eagle's sky
Dive, dive the eagle alive
Glory every cloud with your flight
Leave a fiery trail high above
But do not, do not long for the old
Do not, do not let your mind paddle those silent lakes
Do not, do not run from all the bloody heartbreaks
This, this is the time to let fly
This, this is the time to say goodbye
Chant, chant your rivers sparkling full
Chant, chant your rivers down, down, down to the sea
Chant, chant your heart free,
Chant for every bird and every tree
Chant, chant the Truth of the Great Mystery

This the open ground
This the pure eagle's sound
This, this the breathing Earth
This, this the timeless dream
This, this the crystalline stream
This, this the galloping plains' magic supreme

Take your hurt to where the river is dancing white
Take your past to where the drums beat all night
Take your naked spirit into the firelight
Let your truth raise you tall
Until you can see above your ancient walls
This, this your spirit's door
This, this your farewell to a dead shore
This, this the open ground
This, this the pure eagle's sound
This, this the breathing Earth
This, this the holy day
This, this the invitation that will not go away
This, this the invitation that will not go away

The Seed Stirs In Its Shell

The seed stirs in its shell
Doubting its urge to stretch and swell
Believing the jive of security's spell
Losing faith in the uncoiling of pure green
Again and again reducing real freedom to a fool's dream

And ain't it easy to dress up stagnation
With superficial change and constant occupation
And ain't it easy to pretend we're free
As we redecorate our cage
And ain't no room for sanity
When we forget we're sleeping on stage

The seed stirs in its shell
Trying to think its way into a cosier hell
So afraid to live, and so afraid to die
So afraid to lose face, and so afraid to lose its place
Looking, looking, looking for others with the same excuse

And ain't it easy to dress up stagnation
With superficial change and constant occupation
And ain't it easy to pretend we can see
As we buy ourselves a bigger cage
And ain't no room, ain't no room for sanity
When we forget we're sleeping through every page

The seed stirs in its shell
Needing to sacrifice what it takes to be itself
Needing to trust something deeper than its assumed history
And it's so, so easy to defend,
So, so easy to defend
Against what appears to be the end

And ain't it easy to dress up stagnation
With superficial change and constant occupation
And ain't it easy, ain't it easy to die before we live
And ain't it easy to ignore the knocking on the door
And ain't it easy to bury ourselves at the shore
And ain't it easy to be a frozen wave
And ain't it easy to join everyone else in their mass grave
And still the seed stirs in its shell
And still the seed strains toward the light
Ever looking to leave its wraparound night
O Ride its green impulse, ride it now
Ride it clean, ride it straight,
O Ride it before it's too late
O Ride it before it's too late

Again And Again

Again I break, my need dissolving my pride
Again I spill, my hurt streaming, streaming wide
Again I die, letting grief and joy burst and fly, fly, fly
Again I whisper and roar, swimming through the dreamy door
And again I join what's above with what's below
And again I recognize the one behind the show

Again I sink, dragged down by my craving to think
Again I rise, blazing bright, enrobed with glistening night
Again I awaken, tired of every lucid fascination
Again I reach out to you, my demand not mine, but Thine
And again I join what's above with what's below
And again I recognize the one behind the show

Again I slip, one hand on the candy, the other on a parental whip
Again I seize the wheel, looking for somewhere special to kneel
Again I pump up my will, trying to stake out the Holy Thrill
Again I laugh myself loose, no longer out to buy a refill
And again I join what's above with what's below
And again I recognize the one behind the show

Again I let go, my love outbreathing every me
Again I float alone, my heart aflood with speechless Mystery
Again I kiss you goodbye, while a truer you drinks my Eternal hello
Again I stand solid, letting every upset enrich my earth
And again I join what's above with what's below
And again I recognize the one behind the show

Again I bulge, feeling murder snaking, snaking down my arms
Again I pray, my dungeon walls swallowing my bloody calls
Again I die, releasing all that I took to be mine
Again I exult, bounding through forests of palm and pine
And again I join what's above with what's below
And again I recognize the one behind the show

Again I gaze from one eye, watching my blood cut rivers in the snow
Again I beat a sweating drum, urging you to leave your mind
Again I smile, leading you into the black chamber of psychic trial
Again I dance before blue fire, entombed by mountainous desire
And again I join what's above with what's below
And again I recognize the one behind the show

Again I remember, and open my innermost wounds
Again I remember, and rise where I once lay ruined
Again I am sweet with force, riding wild green waters down to the sea
Again I face my delusion, taking the mind out of my confusion
Again I break and again I die, again I break and again I die
And again I rise and again I awaken
And again I fall, forgetting the Sacred Call
And again I remember, and again I include it all
And again we are here, already free, not to have, but to be,
To form and unform, to be lovers with the calm and the storm
And again I join what's above with what's below
And again I recognize the one behind the show
And again everything's aflame with the Holy Glow,
Again and ever again...

What Is Asked Of Us Is Asked In Every Condition

What is asked of us is asked in every condition
Each moment offers us the same decision
Be a machine, or be a human being

Whatever happens, the demand is the same
We take the jump, or we keep on dishing out blame
Whatever happens, we stand before the same door
We go on through, or we keep on redecorating our snore

What is asked of us is asked in every condition
Hear it, hear it now
Hear it in your next breath
Hear it in the whisper of your death
Hear it, hear it now
Feel it, feel it now
Feel it inside and outside
Feel it beating your heart
Feel it, feel it now
Feel it 'til the dark's in love with the light

Nothing, nothing, nothing is stopping you
Just make the moves you were born to make
Simply practise being awake
What is asked of us is asked in every condition
Each moment offers us the same decision

Be a machine, or be a human being
Be caught in thought, or undo your knot
Be run by mind, or shine through all that is blind
Be false, or be true
Go flatter, or go to the heart of the matter
Go into stagnation, or go beyond all consolation
Reinforce your disguise, or rub the sleep out of your eyes
Be false, or be true
So what will you do?
So what will you do?
Don't listen to the you who asks how
Just take the jump, or let it take you, right now
It is not a jump of ambition, but of open-eyed permission

What is asked of us is asked in every condition
Each moment offers us the same decision
Be a machine, or be a human being
Be false, or be true
So what will you do?
So what will you, what will you, what will you do?

When The Night
Pulled Back The Bedcovers

When the night pulled back the bedcovers
And I sat knees-up lightly ashaking, hoping for a sign sublime
My mind looking for the time,
My body athrob with an eternal rhyme,
The windows, the windows did bulge with something unborn
Something I couldn't name, something I could not contain

O When the night pulled back the bedcovers
And inside and outside were lovers
And exhale was inhale
I did cry out for having so much, and for wanting more,
And for having done all this before

O When the night pulled back the bedcovers
And I rose from the ruins of my dreams
And the dark came rushing in, spilling its stars
I did cry out for having so much, and for wanting more,
And for having done all this before

O When the night pulled back the bedcovers
And my breath was not mine, and I knew the Holy Design
And the dark stormed my room so sweet and so bright
And my spine was a stem of light, so green and so, so white
I did, I did give the night my hand
And let it lead me through every face of every shadowland

O When the night pulled back the bedcovers
And inside and outside were lovers
And exhale was inhale, and I knew a love that could not fail,
A love that was both ocean and sail
I did cry out for having so much, and for wanting more,
And for having done all this before
And still I wait for the great night shining wild
The great night full of child
The great night shining, shining, shining so wild
The great night so full of child
And still I wait for the vast night with its eyes of daylight
An undreaming love so near
Inviting me to abandon my fear
Inviting me to give the night my hand
Until I can look through the eyes
Of every face of every shadowland
And every outside and every inside
Meet in blazing embrace

O Surrounded by womb was I, the walls all aquiver
And new growth running wild and velvet through my room
And my whole being did shiver and shake
Until my frame of mind did break
And I was in body what I was in spirit
The great night shining wild
The great night undefiled
The great night forever full of child

True Spring

Sky's acurl, sky's a dimpling pearl
Plumtrees blossomed plump, round and round
Robins tugging atop the dewbright dawn
Yanking pink spaghetti from the ground

Emerald buds all ashiver, lips moistly aquiver
Spring bursting through Winter's seams
New life sprouting from green dreams
And Spring sings through the stiff and the damp,
Loosening, loosening, loosening Winter's cramp
And Spring wings wild, bringing forth its art,
Blocked only in humankind's dozing heart

There are so, so many marooned from real love
So many who won't fully feel, so many asleep at the wheel
So many stuck in recoil, locked into a frozen soil
So many spraying flowered scenes over their desolation,
Living where doubt and blind faith throw the dice,
Living where Spring seems to be but a fool's dream,
Living where passion's all heat and no light,
Where fear fills the night

False Spring leaps from newsstand covers,
Plastered with the plastic faces of fashionable lovers
False Spring sells potions and notions of rejuvenation,
Offering fantasies of happiness and supercopulation

And it's a dressed-up stagger over ruined land
And it's a desperate painting-over of primal pain
And it's keeping so, so many cosily insane
And it's stuck on giving Winter a Springtime face
And its every action is but distraction
From its self-imposed dissatisfaction
True Spring is not a remedy for Winter
True Spring's wonder is shaped by Winter's icy hand
True Spring rises refreshed from Winter's land
True Spring lets its green current touch all,
Asking only a letting go of the old
Asking only that new life be allowed to unfold
And humankind looks the other way
Dreaming that it's awake, dreaming that it's okay,
Turning true Spring into a children's fable
Making true Spring a storybook ideal,
Only divorcing itself from the green longing
The green longing alive in even the most mind-battered heart
The green longing alive behind even the hardest eye
The green longing shining through even the most crippled cry,
The longing, the longing speechless with pure green
The longing, the longing of forgotten being

One Fine Morning

One fine morning I pulled up, pulled up my roots
I took off my face and leapt, leapt into new boots
My body no longer penned up in my mind
My stride no longer bound by time

REFRAIN: Hello to the high and hello to the low
Hello to the yes and hello to the no
Dance, dance it true, outdance every you
Dance, dance it bright, dance us through the night

One fine morning I said so long, so long to misery
I took down my mirror and taught, taught my flesh to see
No longer, no longer looking for the key in artificial light
No longer, no longer making a problem out of the night

REFRAIN

One fine morning, one fine morning, I took my heart back
I woke up, woke up flying, flying along the right track
No longer, no longer begging for anyone's applause
No longer, no longer turning God into Santa Claus

REFRAIN

One fine morning I began, yes I began, a goodbye
That left nothing to be left, not even, not even the Holy High
Something melted so, so sweet in me, so, so fine
Something I could not name, something I could not claim as mine
A starburst streaming wild it was, shattering the grip of Time,
Rocketing me far beyond the reach of my mind

REFRAIN

One fine morning I laughed and wept away all my rust
I burned my lottery stubs and made friends, friends with my lust
And how, how my love did die into a deeper love,
And how, how my joy did become my ground, not my goal
And how, how natural, natural, natural it is to be whole
No longer, no longer separating body and soul

REFRAIN

One fine morning I held nothing back, nothing from the holy fire
There was nothing to escape from, not even my lowest desire
Every joy and every pain was mine, mine to reveal,
Mine to fully feel
Every up and every down was mine, mine to know, mine to outgrow
And do we not know we cannot buy our way out?
And do we not, do we not know it is folly to stall?
And do we not, do we not already live where there is room for all?
And do we not, do we not see our Truth shining all about?
And are we not, are we not with the One Who outblazes all doubt?
And is not, is not the door open now, open wide?
And is not, is not this longing beyond all pride,
Is it not your purest guide?
This, this longing so, so ready
For you to ride, ride on Home

REFRAIN

I Stand On The Shore

I stand on the raingrey shore
Leaning into the windchilled thrill of daybreak's air
I stand on the rainbowed shore
Until I'm ground to sand, drowned in broken waves,
Spilling shattered against another shore,
My blood the ocean's roar

I stand on the shore
Letting the wind have my face
Letting the dawning day set my pace
Letting the upcurling waves thunder down
Letting the sky cup my heart and melt my crown
Letting the child unfold and the lucid brilliance behold
Letting go the righteous should and the executioner's hood
Letting go the victim's disguise and the sleeper's lies
Letting go and letting go, 'til disillusionment shines through,
Shines on through both the cynic's and the convert's view

And doesn't something whisper: Give me your hidden fear!
And doesn't something sing: Give me your shield and your spear!
And doesn't something shout: Give me your despair and your doubt!
And doesn't, doesn't something cry out: Let me lighten your step!
  Let me, let me brighten your loins! Let me ungirdle your belly
  and undam your chest and unchain your throat and fountainburst
  your skull and look, look, look through your eyes
  until you know beyond any doubt and beyond any proof
  that it's you, you, you looking through it all

And now all my bodies, all my bodies sing so full
The body unbound, the body bright, the body divine,
The dreambody, the everyday body, the body of time,
The embodiment of possibility, flesh of mud and stars,
Flesh of gravity, flesh of ecstasy, flesh of personal history,
Body after body, body within body, all speaking their mind
And still I arise in pure Mystery
Again standing on the rainswept shore
Sky all pierced by pearly tubes of light
Broken waves pouring through all I can see
And I walk on, letting the day undress me
And I walk on, uprooted until I find a truer ground

Inside you and me beats an ocean
Its waves shaping our every shore
Its breath weaving through our every cry
And aren't we so, so near to where love outshines fear,
To where we can only again and again reappear,
Until the Holy Mystery makes itself plain,
And we've nothing, nothing to attain,
Only this Wonder to know,
This Wonder to forever live

I Come To You

I come to you through it all
I am the one, the one who hears your spirit call
I am the one who is sky for your holiest fire
Do not, do not turn from me, even in your darkest desire

REFRAIN: Love me now, love me full
             Love me bright, love me day and night
             I cannot be found, because I cannot be lost
             Love me, love me whatever the cost

I come to you through the high and through the low
I am the one, the one you cannot name, but always know
I am the one who is earth for your purest dance
Do not, do not turn from me, even in your blackest trance

REFRAIN

I come to you through the heart of every now
I am the one, the one for whom there's no why,
But only eternal Thou
I am the one who is ocean for all your streamings
Do not, do not turn from me, even in your densest dreamings

REFRAIN

I come to you in all forms
I am the one, the one throbbing with all storms
I am the one who is fire for what's useless in you
Do not, do not turn from me, no matter how convincing your view

REFRAIN

I come to you when love is sailing free
I am the one, the one you always feel, but cannot just see
I am the one who is space for your deepest loss of face
Do not, do not turn from me, no matter how hard your place

REFRAIN

I come to you when you'll do whatever it takes
I am the one, the one you forget, but cannot forsake
I am the one who breathes you true
Do not, do not turn from me, even when you are solid blue

REFRAIN

I come to you when love is burning bright, burning, burning
I am the one, the one aflame in every sacred site
I am the one rising from the ruins, rising now, rising full
I come to you now, when love is burning bright, burning, burning
O burning, burning clear, burning and burning, burning through to you
To you, to you, to you
Burning awake your deepest yearning,
Until joy's the ground, and love's the power all around,
Until our hearts speak Truth's tongue,
Until our song is fully sung

REFRAIN

Back, Back Goes He

Back, back to the clouds of speechless smoke
Back, back to the charred shock
Back, back to his woman's plundered remains
Back, back to the day too bright
Back, back to the crimson silence
Back, back to the rage that soon must wail
This his son, this his daughter, this his woman
This, this his people, all blackened and frosty red
This, this his tribe, young and old and now so, so cold

Back, back came he, back from forest and plain
Back, back came he, back from spirit-adventure
Back, back came he, back from the single eye
Back, back, with no one here
Where he stands is holy, holy is the ground
Where he stands is holy, holy is the ground
The bodies light his grief and catch his waterfall of pain
Back, back he has come, back to a searing rain
Where he stands is holy, holy is the ground
Where he stands is holy, holy is the ground
His feet find the Earth, his hurt storms open his skull
Back, back to his body goes he, dancing deep and wild
And the spirits of the murdered mourn through his flesh
And together they grieve, together and together until they leave
And alone is he, the night close around, the wind whistling high
Where he sits is holy, holy is the ground
Where he weeps is holy, holy is the sound

A fire gathers in the ruins, burning through the loss
A wreath of blue flames consuming his name
Away steps he, all his goodbyes left in the smoke
Away walks he, through his pain
Away walks he, through his past
Broken is he, broken yet whole, carrying his luminous wound
Where he walks is holy, holy is the land
Where he walks is holy, holy is the land
Back, back goes he, back into the forest dark
Back, back goes he, back to something new
Back, back goes he, back to the Great Waters,
Back to the Open Sky
Back, back goes he, back to a love big enough for all sorrow
Back, back goes he, back to a joy free of every tomorrow
Back, back goes he, back to something new
Back, back goes he, back to embody the Holy View
His woman and children and tribe in his arms
Where he dies is holy, holy is the ground
Where he dies is holy, holy is the ground
Great Spirit all around

Look For Me

Look for me
where storms come uncaged
Look for me
where the sea carries shattered sky
Look for me
where joy and pain disappear into sun and rain,
where we can only once again love ourselves sane

Look for me
where dewdrops make cathedrals out of grass
Look for me
where sunlight fans through throbbing decay
Look for me
where joy and pain disappear into sun and rain,
where we can only once again love ourselves sane

Look for me
where dragonlizards await their prey
Look for me
where epic shields are gripped by laureled hand
Look for me
where emerald valleys sway in orgasmic trance
Look for me
where joy and pain disappear into sun and rain,
where we can only once again love ourselves sane

Look for me
where the land is wild with rhythmed wonder
Look for me
where jagged shores moan with white thunder
Look for me
where the sea is ablaze with dawn
Look for me
where joy and pain disappear into sun and rain,
where we can only once again love ourselves sane

Look for me
where the elements dance and die
Look for me
where forehead is an infinity of sky
Look for me
Inside your looking
Look for me
where joy and pain disappear into sun and rain,
where we can only once again love ourselves sane
Look for me, look for me, look, look, look for me
where we can only dance the sacred dance,
       the dance whose heart beats out of time,
          forever surrendered to an ecstatic Rhyme

Sacred Hymn

O Father of my soul, O Breath of my breath,
Taking me through death after death
O Guide me on, guide me, guide me free,
Guide me, guide me on, guide me into Thee
O May I be a vessel for Your Light
As I sail through the night

REFRAIN: In You I rise and fall,
         My everything pulsing with Your Call
         Ever, ever, ever dying into You am I,
         Like clouds into endless sky

O Mother of my soul, O Cradle of my every birth,
O Green, green heartbeat of my earth,
Your Love the ever-virgin Mystery
O Guide me on, guide me, guide me free,
Guide me, guide me on, guide me into Thee
O May I make room for Your Embrace
And may I awaken to You in every, every place

REFRAIN

O Spring of my soul, O Flame of pure desire,
Is not, is not Your Welcome all that I require?
And do I not, do I not now dance in your Spirit-Fire?
O Guide me on, guide me, guide me free,
Guide me, guide me on, guide me into Thee
O May I open to You, up and down, round and round
Until my heart has found its truest ground

REFRAIN

O Lover of my all, O Joy that cannot die,
O Love that cannot lie,
Are you not forever, forever, forever here?
And is not this how You must now appear?
O Guide me on, guide me, guide me free,
Guide me, guide me on, guide me into Thee
O Great Heart, we are never, never apart
O Great Heart, we are never, never apart
Never, never, never apart
Never, never, never apart
Ever, ever, ever in it together
Every day and in every way
O May I live You full and may I live You now,
My everything remembering, remembering, remembering
    that we are never, never, never apart
Never, never, never apart...

Take Me

Take me to the bottom of your pain
Take me to the weave of your true name
Take me, take me deep, take me steep
Let's stretch to make the leap
Let's go to where love must also weep

Take me to the bottom of your pain
Take me to the weave of your true name
Take me, take me in, take me for a heartspin
Let's live where insights lose their mind
Let's go to where love is never blind

Take me to the bottom of your pain
Take me to the weave of your true name
Take me, take me over the rise,
Take me past all your goodbyes
Let's shine through our every disguise
Let's go to where love's passion can fly

Take me to the bottom of your pain
Take me to the weave of your true name
Take me, take me past your past,
Take me to the end of your hope
Let's stop looking for a better deal
Let's go to where love tells no one to kneel

Take me to the bottom of your pain
Take me to the weave of your true name
Take me, take me in, make me yours, bake me in your sun
Let's throw away our every alibi
Let's go to where love cannot lie

Take me to the bottom of your pain
Take me to the weave of your true name
Take me, take me to us, take me beyond all the fuss
I am your oldest ally, I am your sky's deepest cry
I am the hello in your grief,
I am the joy of each new leaf
I am your oldest ally, I am, I am your sky's deepest cry
I am the hello in your grief
And I am, I am the joy of each new leaf
I am the lord of your stride
I am the one for whom you have always cried

Take me to the bottom of your pain
Take me to the weave of your true name.
Take me, take me deep, take me steep
Let's stretch to make the leap
Let's go to where love must also weep
Take me, take me in, take me through your hidden door
Take me, take me all the way, take me right to your core
Take me, take me all the way, take me right to your core
Let's throw away our every alibi
Let's go to where love cannot lie

Give Me Your Hand

Give me your hand
And let me show you my land
Come with me high above the timberline
Come breathe the snowy air
There are flowers circling every peak
There's a perfume clear as it's sweet

Give me your eye
And let me show you my sky
Come with me into the shining night
Come let exploding stars deepen your delight
There are unborn storms and blue-armed glories
There is a brilliance throbbing inside

Give me your heart
And let me show you my deepest art
Come with me into the one-eyed cave
Come let every passion birth the Holy Wave
There are allies all around
There is a joy forever calling for you

Give me your point of view
And let me show you what you always knew
Come with me into the Unknowable Now
Come let wonder widen your brow
There are children whose wombs wait for you
There is a land where your mind cannot go

Give me your all
And let me show you the door through the wall
Come with me into the heart of the fire
Come leap speechless into open-eyed desire
There are countless faces of endless Mystery
There is an understanding dancing free

Give me this
And let me show you your bliss
Come with me into every room
Come let the sobering joy bloom
Give me this
Give me what you most miss
Is it not time to receive Eternity's Kiss?

Part IV

Welcoming The Preparatory Fire

27

You Are Being Tested, Now

Our every circumstance, inner and outer, presents a test for us. If we pass it, we move toward, or reinforce our move toward, a more fitting level of being, a deeper resonance with Truth, a more full-blooded embodiment of all that we are. If we fail, we stay where we are, or, if failure has been unnaturally prolonged or indulged, we regress, losing all sense that we are even being tested, again and again exploiting our capacity for playing victim to circumstances, ever maintaining our slumber, except perhaps when some crisis or nightmare momentarily shocks us into awareness.

Our testing is not being administered by some omnipresent Somebody, but is spontaneously generated by what we are doing with our true needs — our very actions and reactions keep setting in motion corresponding forces that both reflect and exaggerate our current condition. Being tested is a matter of multidimensional gravitation, or attraction of conditions, personified or not, that precisely fit our real needs. If we're out of touch with such needs, then what comes our way in the form of testing will seem to us to be alien, unfair, bad luck, or even a complete surprise.

Also, our testing has nothing whatsoever to do with typical evaluation — there is no built-in degradation for failing to "make the grade". Everyone must learn at their own rate, and in their own way, not the "own" of their persona, but the "own" of their core of being. Those of us who repeatedly suffer the same failure simply because of our unswerving commitment to remaining blind are, unknown to ourselves, only inviting in bigger and bigger crises, or vastly overblown tests, the very intensity of which almost invariably matches the intensity of our denial about what's really happening. If such crises are not sanely responded to, as evidenced by some degree of waking up and changing what must be changed, then we will all too easily tend to settle into a done-to stance for the rest of our life, mechanically pointing an accusing finger at our supposedly unfavourable circumstances, not seeing that such situations actually provide ideal conditions for liberation, or awakening...

Success is basically no more than the making good use of our failures. This is not about a gloried solidification of everyday self, but rather about dissolution of (and disidentification with) that very self. It is about losing face without losing touch. It is about giving our all without giving ourselves away. There is no applause, no boos, no Santa Claus, but only the emerging fullness of who we are. Clearly recognizing our continuing failure to wake up is the beginning, along with the full-bodied realization that what is being avoided is *exactly* where we must go.

Earth is a school, a place of transition, a wondrous crucible of evolutionary possibility. Its lessons are to be consciously embodied and fully lived. If we try to escape from Earth's demands, whether through indulgence of appetite, or through egoic consolation, or through distracting dramatizations of our suffering, or through meditative remedies, then we only make ourselves more and more impotent relative to our testing.

There are no shortcuts. There is simply a demand to be met, now.

The point is not to reach some superworld, some heavenly version of Earth, some subtle realm where we don't have to feel pain. The point is to freely embrace our Earth-life, to live it with passion and sensitivity and wakefulness, to breathe it right to our center of being, to cradle its joy and its grief, to turn away from none of it, until we *naturally* pass through it, until we are cleanly free of all fascination with it and its possibilities, until we are no longer bound or obsessed by it. To try to reach this freedom through mere allegiance to therapeutic, religious, psychic, or mental strategies only strands us in a quicksand of goal-fixation. It *all* must be passed through, directly and nakedly, without clinging to dogma, belief, spiritual ambition or any other buffer. Purification, however fiery, must eventually be *welcomed*. Discipline is necessary, but it is of no use if its origin is egocentric. Sooner or later, joy must become the *foundation* of our journey, rather than its goal — if we're hoping that our passage will make us feel better, then we will be undertaking it for the wrong reason, doing no more than crippling ourselves with unnecessary expectation.

Nothing must be flinched from. It *all* must be felt, right to the heart, every last fibre of it, every in and out of it, every glory and every horror, felt with pure vulnerability and openness of eye, without any emotional dissociation. Awakening must become more important to us than sedation. Our wounds must be exposed, not morbidly, but with heart-felt honesty and humour, with lust and subtlety, with guts and sensitivity, until a sobering joy blooms, until we are rooted in the primal rhythms of the moment, free of all hope. We are constantly being tested in a manner that *exactly* reveals what we are flinching from. Look, and see. What are you now recoiling from? What are you now postponing? What are you now talking yourself out of? Be grateful that it is right before you, right now...

28

Guilt Means
We Don't Have To Grow

Guilt is not a feeling, but a suppression of feeling, a psychophysical knottedness, a mind-induced collapse of heart, a deep splitting of self that allows us to *continue* doing whatever it is that apparently makes us "feel" guilty — guilt's domain is one of unresolved parent-child conflicts, a habitually stalemated world in which we can simultaneously "do it" and punish ourselves for so doing.

Guilt means we get to stay small.

It is a refusal to live without parental authority, not the parental authority native to ourselves, but rather that of those who rigidly demand and propagandize for our allegiance or membership.

Guilt means we don't have to grow.

It safeguards our immaturity by exploiting our craving for security; in the perverse cosiness of its murky, stagnant waters, we drift in utterly predictable circles, finding an endarkened safety, however miserable, in such repetitive familiarity, all the while exhausting our vitality and marooning ourselves from love, especially our own.

Guilt reduces God to the Ultimate Parent, thereby filling churches and emptying hearts and pockets. It can often be seen masquerading as conscience.

Guilt's protagonists, the child who obsessively "does it," and the parent who wields the righteous whip, cannot escape each other; they not only breathe the same air, but look through the same eyes.

Guilt is a superimposition on our being, a psychological parasite that we allow to feed on us, and it is also *our* activity, something *we* are doing to ourselves, something *we* are insisting on fleshing out...

And guilt is but frozen shame. Guilt's morality is based on blame, whereas shame's is rooted in responsibility. Amplified guilt is but torture, but amplified shame, when skilfully worked with, is purification, emotional release, self-forgiveness, a full-blooded return to wholeness, a warmly streaming catharsis of the entire body and mind, carrying us past all blame. Healthy shame carries within itself not only a heartfelt acknowledgment of what was done, but also a richly pulsating capacity for true expansion...

Guilt is but a confession of being stuck. It is just a habit, just the mechanical resurrection of unhealed parent-child conflicts and stand-offs, just a childhood souvenir seemingly demanding animation.

To cut through guilt, don't take either of its sides. They are but clouds, however dark or compelling. Be their sky. Introduce them, unmask them, bridge them, bring them together, letting their mutual rainburst be your cry...

29

Conformity And Individuality

Conformity is obsessive attachment to form, inner or outer. Penetrate the usual human's display of individuality, and you will find yourself in a quicksand of unquestioning submission to an ethical complex utterly bereft of awakening's morality. Go deeper, and you'll encounter that person's real individuality, straining for release and expression, burdened by intense, paranoid opposition from what is peripheral to it. This depth, this suppressed uniqueness, is commonly viewed as untrustworthy, savage, and irresponsible, needing incarceration or well-policed constraints for society's good. Yes, when it is let out, it often does behave as predicted by societal overseers, but only because of the aberrating effect of having been penned up for so long, without love or conscious attention. Thus do we reinforce and thicken our superficiality, compulsively painting it deep, generating through our repressive violation of our individuality a realm writhing with the forces of war, suspicion, loneliness, dread, hypocrisy, and anaesthetizing distraction...

We tend to be fascinated by extreme non-conformists, both condemning and glorifying them, seeing in them our own urge to break form, but not seeing that almost all of them are conforming to the rules of their nonconformity, clinging to it with all the tenacity of any suburban mole. The obedient citizen plays child to the State; the disobedient citizen plays adolescent. Both are bound to the parental force of the State, one positively, one negatively. Both define freedom in terms of their relationship to their particular society; neither is willing to stand their true ground.

And what of the longing to transcend all conformity, to not make a prison out of form, but rather a luminous cocoon, a heartfelt acceptance and celebration of limitation? We cannot escape from form, but we can purify our attachment to form. Avoiding attachment does not bring about liberation, but only the illusion of liberation. Those who would flee all form, whether through psychotic dissociation or yogic strategies (such as meditative absorption in the formless dimension of Existence), are but spitting upon God as Manifestation, shrinking from their inherent intimacy with all that is...

Conformity encourages addiction to repetition, thus militating against real spontaneity, reducing play to a pseudo-uninhibitedness that is neither sensitive nor subtle. Such play is basically a waste of energy, a handy outlet for discharging the surface-level distress created by conformity — it is psychological masturbation, an enervating emptying of one's overtensed vitality. Watch people interact, really watch, watch with open eyes, watch from center, and see the suppressed hurt and need, see the remote-control recitations, the compulsively dramatized pain, the deadening familiarity, the loophole lies, the well-scrubbed disguise, the broken children weeping unheard — see, really see, the commitment to playing it safe, see the crushed longing for love struggling to get through, see the misguided loyalty to persona zipping up face after face, see the moment-to-moment murder of the awakening impulse, see the fake individuality, the robotic resignation, the suffocating despair, the mechanical good cheer, the fear of fear...

Realization of our individuality is not arrived at through conformity, nor is it arrived at through a flaunting of conformity. Such realization may even wear the clothes of conformity, but it is free, completely untrapped by its embracing of its particular limits. It is not trying to look individualistic; it is not trying to be special, for it is already intimate with its own uniqueness. Before it goes out in public, it brushes its hair and buttons its shirt, at ease with both its radiance and its anonymity.

Individuality is naturally responsible, naturally functional, naturally loving. It gives attention, rather than demanding it. It honours form as much as it honours formlessness.

It is not concerned with fitting in, because it already has an unexploitable sense of belonging to That Which animates all. It is secure in its bittersweet celebration of the inherent insecurity of Life. It does not fear Death. It turns away neither from grief, nor from ecstasy. It is what grows from center; its garden is ours to tend. It moves in and out of conformity with fluid ease, hiding nothing, yet revealing only what corresponds to the level of being of whomever it is addressing. It breathes us true. It loves, and loves ruthlessly. Its aspects work together, harmoniously. It is ready for the unexpected. It loses face without losing touch. It gives its love without giving itself away. It is *present*, even behind the most mind-battered heart. It is the seed having cracked its shell beyond repair, the seed having fully surrendered to the uncoiling of pure green. It knows exactly what to do, and when to do it. Even now, it beats in us, inviting our undivided attention...

30

The "New Age"
Is A False Awakening

Almost all of us have experienced false awakenings during our dreams, thoroughly convincing ourselves that we were definitely awake, only to later realize that we were actually still dreaming; this realization, however, takes place not in the dreaming state (with the exception of "lucid" dreams), but in the so-called waking state. False awakenings, by presupposing that we were just dreaming, but aren't now, do demonstrate a slight, albeit confusing, distance from the dreaming process, an embryonic witnessing, an almost-budding awareness throbbing with its potential. Unfortunately, very few of us use, or even consider using, our false awakenings as steppingstones into true awareness.

When we settle for a surrogate of real wakefulness, we are even less available to the awakening impulse than when we are simply dreaming without any notion whatsoever that we might have been dreaming. This is exactly paralleled in the daytime sleep known as the waking state. The small percentage of those who have some sense that such sleep is occurring all too often only separate themselves from the mechanized madness around them just enough to have opinions about it, or contrary ideologies, but not far enough to truly enter the domain of wakefulness. Righteously cementing themselves into their false awakening, they busy themselves bleating about the problems of the world and about "higher" values, wholistic paradigms, the emergence of a new consciousness, and all sorts of "healing", ever expressing and defending a morality that will apparently take care of everything, if only the sleeping hordes will listen, believe, and thus transform the planet...

This morality, however, is but mind-made. Inflated by the zeal of its converts, it purports to stem forth from Love, Truth, and Harmony with God, but in fact is only a complex *abstraction* of these, an idealism firmly impaled upon hope, ever nostalgic for the future. In our time, this is epitomized by what is termed the "New Age." With its rigid good cheer, cosmic parrotings, superficiality, fake spirituality, addiction to metaphysical consolation, and obsession with gentleness, safety, and emotional sedation, the "New Age" is a gross parody of human integrity and awakening, a glossy institutionalization of false awakening. "New Age" devotees glibly talk of "unconditional" love, not seeing that they have merely *abstracted* love, reducing it to an ideal, an idol of mind, while their capacity for real love withers from lack of attention. As for Truth, they've reduced it to information, to factual lifelessness, not realizing that Truth cannot be pickled and presented to tomorrow, that Truth is alive, always fresh, spontaneous, and unrehearsable. "New Age" followers try to *mentally* catapult themselves into Truth's realm, instead of whole-heartedly living it and embodying it with no reservation, welcoming whatever fires it brings them.

The "New Age" is a desert of religious lullabies, cluttered by mirages of mind, greened by idealism's imaginary oases, mistaking its sandstorms of grandiose thought for revelation. The "New Age" is also escapism of the most cowardly kind, escape from the demand that pain and suffering be truly faced, embraced, and passed through, rather than just risen above, or seemingly dissolved by mental manipulation. Like any other rigorously entrenched false awakening, the "New Age" assumes it has a true overview, a clear vision, but it cannot even see itself — it speaks of oneness, of unity, of nondualism, yet it chronically divides everything into positive and negative, making a virtue out of the former, and fleeing the latter, not realizing that such avoidance only further deforms and endarkens those passions labelled as "negative," thereby leaving them so repressed and unloved (the very distress of doing so being robotically discharged through compulsive sexing and/or mentalizing) as to be but unavailable Life-Energy, marooned from their real purpose.

It is no accident that so many "New Age" adherents are shallow, emotionally impoverished, and terminally nice — they are terrified to truly become whole, to truly heal themselves, to truly illuminate and embrace their woundedness, because to do so would necessitate their going into their darkness and getting right to the heart of it, not from a distance, but first-hand, regardless of the consequences. They'd rather think and think about such a journey, romanticizing it, making believe they *are* doing it, that they *are* engaged in it, desperately believing that there doesn't have to be pain and suffering, not noticing that their clinging to such belief is only creating *more* pain and suffering for them.

In most cases, the more they hurt, the more fanatical they become about their beliefs, preaching about oneness, the dawning of a new consciousness, and "us-ness," glibly lying about their festering misery, exaggeratedly and unconsciously acting out the turning away from authenticity that we all carry within ourselves, the turning away that all too many of us align ourselves with, while our spirit weeps unheard, ever calling to us, ever inviting us to reclaim our native integrity of being...

The "New Age" is over.

It has become a dead system, doing no more than sucking energy from its devotees. Its little stream, with all its big ideas, has all but been absorbed into the voracious mainstream of our culture, trivialized into instant stardom and instant oblivion, gobbled up like any other bowlful of colourful information and offbeat entertainment. Nevertheless, what brought the "New Age" into existence still lives, as it always has, whatever its latest appearance, drawing sustenance from every false awakening that is not recognized and undone, especially those strengthened by mass-agreement.

The assumption that we are actually awake must be *tested*, right in the midst of our presumption of wakefulness. This is not easy. Effort is required. The impulse to awaken must be located, embodied, and nourished. The signs of false awakening must be recognized; otherwise, we will only be forming a mini-version of the "New Age" for ourselves, ever knotting ourselves in submission to our false awakening, blindly holing up in its "headquarters," thinking that we are free, even as we kill time doing our time.

It is not even enough to dream lucidly, to *know* that we are dreaming while we are dreaming, unless such lucidity arises without any egocentrically-generated preprogramming. The desire to be "lucid" during a dream, to be a *somebody* who can lucid-dream, creates the very same difficulties as the desire to be awake during the so-called waking state, to be a *somebody* who can meditate or be aware. If meditation, or dream-lucidity, is held in place by some technique or method, some sort of dissociative focus, then it is not pure, nor natural, but only a strategy of mind. Nor is it full awakening, however luminous it might be, for the "somebody" at the center of it is very rarely seen for who they actually are. Not often do lucid dreamers recognize that the them who stars in their lucid dream is but *part* of the dream, no more than a convincing *personification* of the witnessing of the dream. Again, as in false awakenings, there is a tendency to rigidly position ourselves, to take a premature stand, to put down roots where there is no soil, to make real estate out of a moment of light.

It is fine to rest when we've reached a plateau, but it's a waste of time to build a home there. When we are sufficiently rejuvenated, we must go on, or we will spiritually atrophy; our environment, inner and outer, must remain pliable, permeable, and resonant with our degree of awakening. Here there are no fixed rules, no ideology, no earth-saving complexes, no need for an overriding morality, simply because real awakening creates its own morality, a mind-free ethic needing no decoding.

The commitment to awakening is an ongoing act of our entire being. If it arises only in part of us, then it is not authentic, but only the banner of that particular aspect, or layer, of us, no more than a pseudo-spiritual inner patriotism, already armed against possible insurrection from the rest of us. Real commitment doesn't make an enemy out of resistance to it, but rather makes room for it, so that the very energy of resistance to the awakening process becomes but unshackled Life-Energy. Real commitment is the stride of one's totality; it is not forced, but entered into, with a passion that springs not from stimulation, but from love. It is activated when we go deeper than our daily sleep, deeper than our false awakenings, deeper than our programmed lucidity. Such commitment is not duty, nor a "should," nor an amalgam of "good" resolutions, nor a burden, but rather an utterly natural, joyously challenging undertaking, a heartfelt acceptance of responsibility, as well as a full-bodied knowingness that such responsibility is the ground of real freedom...

As long as we act as if the "New Age" or anything else of similar origin is a viable option for us, then we are only tourists relative to the awakening process, fans of God-Communion, mere dilettantes, mistaking enthusiasm for depth, information for Truth, and the emotions associated with positive thinking for Love.

False awakenings are but potential steppingstones. Use them as such.

31

Devotees, Enemies, Tolerators, & Allies Of Spiritual Teachers

Devotees of spiritual teachers are looking to dissolve their boundaries, rather than to expand them, repetitiously whoring themselves for blissful sensations and cultic cosiness, struggling to convince themselves that all is well — they are but children addicted to keeping the houselights on, averting their gaze from all but the most benign of shadows. With glib enthusiasm, they equate ego with individuality, enrolling themselves in programs supposedly designed to eradicate ego, again and again numbing their suspicions with swooning romanticism, airtight jargon, and preverbal regression, lightly tossing aside criticism, including their own, as nothing more than "resistance" or "negativity." They crave the teacher's attention.

And then there are those who automatically oppose or dismiss spiritual teachers, posting guards at their outposts, letting no one in all the way, trusting no one with their undressed heart. Their expansiveness is but empire-building, no more than a cunning stretching and embellishment of egocentricity — they are but adolescents deifying independence, too lost to lose face, looking to corner the market for a convincing substitute for the core of being they have abdicated and forgotten. Trusting only their mistrust, they console themselves with irony, cynicism, hip consumerism, electronic stimulation, and *personalized* conformity. They secretly crave the teacher's attention.

And then there are those who claim to honour all paths, righteously making a virtue out of their phony tolerance — they are but dilettantes, committed to superficiality and *disembodied* reasonableness. Their pretense of understanding and non-judgmentalness merely obscures their fear of taking a real stand. They like to paint wheels on their inertia, depth on their fence-sitting, and humanitarianism on their compulsive mentalizing. Their game is neither neurotic submission, nor neurotic independence, but neurotic peace-making. Terminally nice are they, preferring mediation to participation. They are terrified of real attention, wanting only the kind of attention that focuses just on their opinions, beliefs, and schemes to better the human condition.

Finally, there are those who have the guts and heartfelt intelligence to both recognize and make good use of authentic spiritual teachers. They know how to surrender without being childish, and how to deepen their individuality without being adolescent, and how to broaden their view without diluting their integrity. They are not looking for immunity, nor are they looking to numb themselves. They do not make God into a parent, nor into an idea, nor into a religion.

Happiness is not their goal, but their discipline. Their expansion serves not to accumulate, but to include. They give the teacher their attention, without giving themselves away.

The devotee wants to give someone else the control. The adolescent wants to be in control. The tolerator doesn't want to see who's in control. The lover doesn't make a problem out of control, being already unexploitable.

Lovers know how to surrender without betraying themselves. They know how to stand strong without being rigid. They know how to empower their witness without losing the depth or intensity of their feeling. They are only here, potently and magnificently here, existing both as teacher and student, both child and elder, both surface and depth, learning to welcome every initiatory fire, learning to embody the Truth of every desire, learning to enjoy reaching for every true teaching...

32

Guru-Worship,
Cultism, & God-Communion

Guru-worship is fundamentally no more than spiritual laziness, just one more "solution" to a primarily problematic orientation toward Life. It is but a strategy to anaesthetize oneself to one's difficulties, a strategy to be parented and consoled to such a degree that one's troubles appear to fade, perhaps even seeming to dissolve in a kind of pseudo-bliss remarkably similar to that sought by more worldly types in their pursuit of "good" feelings, ego-reinforcement, and stress-discharge, through compulsive sexual activity. Though guru-worshippers may not act sexually indulgent, at least outwardly, they are just as fucked-up as their more everyday counterparts, repetitiously and fervently masturbating before their airbrushed pinup of God, namely their beloved guru, rubbing themselves blind, making a minor deity out of the juiciest rhythm, stimulating themselves to the point where some sort of release is inevitable, then, infantile, sentimentalized then, pouring forth gushily exaggerated thanks to their guru for their sensations of relief, especially if such sensations resemble those of orgasm.

For devotees, this is love, a love supreme, whereas in fact it is only romance, a romance whose dramatic tension, or erotic promise, is held in place by the very *distance* that such adulation (and craving for oneness) creates, a distance that devotees, in their bhakti intoxication, robotically fantasize into non-existence, just like swooning honeymooners.

Romance depends for its continuation on two simultaneous events: one, the general unavailability of the beloved for *true* intimate contact, and two, the momentary, or fantasized, availability of the beloved for what is assumed to be intimacy (which is little more than a chestful of lust). In other words, romance sustains itself better from a distance, whether physical or emotional — zoom toward the beloved for a real closeup, right into zits, pits, and sagging tits, right into stubble, trouble, and psychic rubble, and the bubble might burst, exposing the whole syrupy charade, especially the devotee's lust for wraparound security and sedation, replete with religious lullabies. Of course, devotees do sometimes have upclose meetings (darshans), however brief or formalized, with their guru, but rarely see anything more than the all-pervading parental projection in which they have swathed their guru, that projection that gives them the biggest, most satisfying sensations of inner swooning and outer belonging... Family, a family that truly works, family...

Guru-worship is an attempt not only to resurrect the feelings, or desired feelings, of infantile bonding and non-discriminating identification with one's original source of sustenance (Mommy or Family), but also to so amplify them that one feels more and more immune to the demands and presence of the world, as well as to the endarkened pain of one's own fragmentation of being. This is no solitary effort, as in early childhood, but is ordinarily a communal effort of all those worshipping the same guru, and therefore has the power of numbers, of mass-agreement, the power of make-believe wholeness.

Power, contrary to popular opinion, does not corrupt, but only exposes what is already corruptible, such as the craving of the devotee, or potential devotee, to fit in somewhere, to belong, to be part of something seemingly bigger than himself or herself, something overflowing with a sense of extended family. Only those of us who already have a strong, well-embodied feeling of belonging to Life Itself are unexploitable by both the self-aggrandizing pull of guru-worship *and* its opposite, the (primarily Western) deification of independence, precisely because we "have" a center of being, a primal and conscious sense of interrelatedness with all that is, whether manifest or unmanifest. Those of us without center, or with poorly defined center, are without any steadiness of resonance with the Essence of Life, so we busy ourselves trying to minimize or numb our resulting sense of insecurity, our profoundly alienating lack of grounding and spirit-connection, by making an all-consuming lifestyle either out of early childhood, as in guru-worship (or unquestioning loyalty to any parental or authoritative force), or out of adolescence, as in the isolationist independence typical of so-called adulthood.

Guru-worship is the epitome of childish irresponsibility. Its adherents glibly bleat about faith, trust, and ego-transcendence, but they've no true faith in themselves, nor any real trust in their capacity to stand their own ground, and their egos are not nearly developed enough, let alone known, to be transcended. Nor do they realize that there is nothing more egotistical than spiritual ambition — the ego loves to paint itself beatific, or put on devotional robes and have its very own guru (who's almost invariably viewed as the greatest guru of all), and then refer to itself as atman, soul, Universal Self, Radiant Transcendental Being, inner Truth, and so on, sometimes even, in a fit of romantic masochism, calling itself "nothing!"

Ego, which is obsessive and unconscious identification with one's personality, is a voracious consumer, appropriating whatever it can from all realms, including the spiritual, so as to ever reinforce its central notion that it really does exist as a discrete entity unto itself, like a little god, a little center of belief, all athrill with its self-serving doctrine of monotheism. Guru-worshippers habitually make an adversary out of ego, blaming it for their failure to perfectly fulfill their guru's demands. However, all ego really needs is the illumination of conscious attention, not so that it will disappear, but so that it will serve and accurately reflect one's depths, rather than just obstruct their expression. Most guru-worshippers are quite egotistical about looking non-egotistical, again and again binding themselves with fake piety and humility, plastering joy and acceptance, or ardent seriousness, all over their faces, running around "serving" others, oozing plastic compassion, earnestly saying that it's all the Guru's Grace, and isn't it wonderful, wonderful, wonderful, to be able to bleat, eat, meet, and excrete so near his or her lotus feet?

Guru-worshippers have not tilled the soil from which real transformation can occur, simply because they don't value such work — it is too *ordinary* for them, too mundane, too conventional, too lowly, too impure, far too full of negativity and unspiritual tendencies. Instead of recognizing that this apparent undesirableness is the very stuff they must face, integrate, and pass through, they avoid it, going around it, or rising above it, feverishly devoting themselves to their guru, hoping that their devotion will somehow absolve them of having to directly face their inner darkness (which includes the decidedly non-spiritual motive that first brought them to their guru).

In rejecting, or refusing to love, what they take to be negative in themselves, they cut themselves off from much of their passion, as well as from their capacity for self-integration, madly compensating for their rigid partiality of being by shacking up with surrogate wholeness, as personified by the Guru. Devotees give as much of their attention as they can to the Guru, braying about how great the Guru is, how at one with God the Guru is, how the Guru is identical to one's true self, how the Guru can do no wrong, how the Guru is all-knowing, how everything the Guru does is for the sake of devotees, and on and on, almost all of it no more than self-rejection. Guru-worshippers readily abandon their critical faculties, especially relative to their guru, prostrating themselves with spineless regularity, mistaking their occasional intensity of emotion for real ecstasy, or, more commonly, acting as if such emotional connection to the Guru is actually occurring.

Doing the opposite is of no more use, however. Sitting back all buttoned-up, playing scientist or cynic, only leaves one immersed in self-verifying doubts, marooned from one's depths and vulnerability, locked up, so to speak, in one's headquarters, just like a frightened adolescent, trying to *think* one's way through everything. To make good use of a guru-figure, legitimate or not, we must have a solid yet fluid center of being, or else we will simply react to the Guru either like a neurotic child or like a neurotic adolescent, slipping either into a romantic dissolution of personal boundaries, or into a paranoid cementing of them.

Guru-worship is a disease, a perversion of our longing for God. It seems to offer an easy way to the Source of All, if we will only faithfully follow its dictates, making the Guru the center of our universe (thereby only going from ego-centered to Guru-centered, a step that is actually but ego-*inflation*). But there are no real shortcuts, only cultic detours and cul-de-sacs strewn with the rotting remains of devotional effort. God-Realization is not a matter of devotion, but of awakening, not monkish, emotionally dissociative awakening, but rather heartfelt, gutsy, full-bodied awakening, alight with an unswerving commitment to getting to the heart of the matter, regardless of the consequences. It is not some kind of ultimate escape, but an end to all escape. It demands nothing less than our totality, our conscious embodiment of all that we are, positive and negative, gross and subtle, big and small, profound and trivial, finite and infinite...

On the other hand, guru-worship, though it promises God-Realization for the faithful, only *seems* to demand our all — yes, it may ask devotees to give up everything, to renounce this and that, to surrender, to be "nothing," but it does not ask them to give up guru-worship, nor their obsession with belonging. Their conformity is precisely the conformity that plagues humanity, the compulsive fitting-in to mind-made morality that so efficiently churns out "good" citizens, each with their very own customized personality and uninhabited core of being. Yes, the Guru may claim a higher ethic, one straight from the Lord of Creation, but the name of the game is still neurotic conformity, maintained by threats, spoken or unspoken, of spiritual harm if one strays from the path.

The implication of "bad karma" for leaving or weaning oneself from guru-worship is no different than that of those societal taboos that say no to ever *truly* leaving one's parents, or to ever outgrowing all of one's conditioning. The enforcing of loyalty to, or "honouring" of, one's parents only makes one perfect material for guru-worshipping — the Guru seems to be the supreme parent, a wondrous enlargement of Mommy and Daddy, a twinkling, all-pervading marvel dwelling in a tax-exempt holy land, or perhaps a cuddly old rascal, an all-loving grandparent with candy in one hand and aphorisms in the other. Of course, the Guru may appear in many other forms besides those of Eastern asceticism and excess — the superstar evangelist, the masterfully packaged mega-musician, the Pope, the head bureaucrat of a psychospiritual seminar business, the corpse-like meditation master, the charismatic or legendary expert, the philandering celibate, the backwoods swami, the latest California avatar, the New Age channeled entity, and on and on. Many of these are joking matters among ordinary people, whose commonsense sniffs out fakery and hype in bigger-than-life parenting, but not in the twisted, unilluminated parenting they themselves have internalized, with all of its unexamined, "should"-infested directives ...

Everyone who is without center is involved in guru-worship, whether their beloved is pontificating upon some vast stage, or is giving discourses in a cave, or is simply spouting forth from inside their skulls; the voice they enslave their ear to promises all sorts of rewards for unquestioning obedience, rewards that include parental approval and "love" (for introverts, extroverts, and converts, of all persuasions, religious or not), God's phone number, and an unlimited expense account in Heaven, Nirvana, Valhalla, or Krishna's Backyard, not to mention bliss, rapture, and ultimate enlightenment. Perform perfectly, and get perfectly transformed or rewarded, and yet still be *you*, good old you, familiar old you, now the ultimate achiever, the first one on the block to realize God — this is the great dream of egocentricity, the goal it craves, the goal from which we unknowingly hang ourselves, ever strangled by our ambition.

Thus do we allow our egocentricity to perpetuate itself, to colonize our depths, to project itself and its vision everywhere, to so absorb us as to leave us all but oblivious to our awakening impulse. But let us remember that ego is not some independent character running around ruining our lives, but rather is something *we* are doing, something we, almost all of the time, are unwittingly pumping energy and attention into. Ego is simply a habit gone to mind, or, put another way, it is the personification of our suppression of being, a collage of entrapping assumptions that repetitiously insists on referring to itself as a somebody, namely us.

Egocentricity not only guru-worships, thus glamourizing itself by association with a seemingly unsurpassed parent-deity, but also is itself the *object* of guru-worship, not by others, but by one's own misguided attention — thus does ego sit upon the throne of self, faking individuality, reinforcing its rule through the subjugation of attention, passion, and Life-force to its imperatives. Such is the primary inner activity of one who is asleep to their true condition, silently suffocating in the deadly masquerade of unexplored ego...

It is easy to make fun of guru-figures, but not so easy to recognize an authentic spiritual teacher, let alone a fully Awakened being. Typical humans, in the name of apparent democracy and egalitarianism, are addicted to reducing everyone to their level of being, resenting those who seem to be definitely superior or more highly evolved, especially those without a "respectable" or societally-approved lineage, ever denouncing them as ego-maniacs, charlatans, false Messiahs, brainwashers, or fools, not realizing that if Christ, Buddha, Lao Tzu, or Socrates were alive today, they would receive exactly the same condemnation as any other guru-figure, if they dared to speak and radiate their wisdom.

The awakened human stands outside the trap of sleeping humanity, inviting one and all to come out, to stand their true ground, but the sleepers are so addicted to their cage that they turn away from their would-be liberators, murdering them in their thoughts (or even literally), again and again rearranging and redecorating their cages, perhaps saving up to buy a bigger or better or more attractively-positioned one, or else dreaming of a heavenly one where they can do just as they please, forever and ever. Guru-worship is a bargaining for such heavenly opportunity and licence, whether its focus is a guru, or some other authority-figure, or is just a particularly upright "should" jammed into a pulpit somewhere behind one's forehead. However, a real spiritual teacher does not console, but awakens humans, offering not a better dream, nor the perfect fulfillment of one's dreams, but rather the possibility of truly awakening from *all* dreams, including the dream of getting enlightened. Such a person may appear as a guru-figure (at least outwardly), or may not at all...

To further flesh out the issue of guru-worship, let us now look at some guru-figures, beginning with Bhagwan Shree Rajneesh. When he began his work, he clearly demonstrated that his approach was no mere parroting of past technique and dogma, but rather a brilliantly original undertaking, designed to both shock and invite people into alertness; he was not, at least initially, some cultic figure, some icon of detachment, but a passionate, intensely creative man, afire with transformative vision, a man obviously awakened beyond his mind. In 1974, he began his Poona ashram, where he soon created a synthesis of Western psychotherapies, cathartic meditations, and Eastern approaches to mindfulness, all of which he enriched and illuminated with daily discourses on a vast range of topics. He had depth, great humour, and an unmistakable radiance of presence. His ashram grew rapidly, attracting more and more seekers — it was a juicy environment, sexy and wild, full of silent flowering and outrageous song, lush with the scent and colour of India, churning with human breakdown and breakthrough...

And it was also a place of tremendous insecurity, both healthy and unhealthy, a hotbed of instant relationships, false intimacies, and glib dismissals of "resistance" to Bhagwan and his ashram, a place of mass conformity to a precisely defined non-conformity, a place where almost everything that happened, especially the needlessly harmful or insensitive, was simplistically viewed as just a "device" (or a deliberate strategy to enhance awakening). As the years flamed by, there were more and more "devices," more institutional abuses, and increasingly intense pressure to fit in, to toe the party line, especially if one wanted to get closer to Bhagwan, who had become much more remote as the number of his devotees multiplied.

His Poona ashram was a cauldron of teeming humanity, a prison for some, a brothel for some, a hide-out for many, and a place of liberation, however superficial, for others. One could sink in it, one could conform to it in the name of "surrender," one could fight it, one could praise it, one could condemn it, or one could make good use of it. Its six acres offered an incredible range of opportunities for those who came not to join, but to plunge into their depths. It was the LSD of spiritual movements, presenting the high and the low with dazzling force and abundance, centered by a man who was obviously overflowing with spirit-force and love.

Guru-worship ran rampant in Poona, but so did human breakthrough. Sadly, far too much of such suddenly naked feeling and spirit-receptivity was used to turn out devotees — the openness generated in therapy groups and in deep meditation (as well as in the social interactions of the ashram) was all too often only viewed as openness to Bhagwan, and therefore reduced to little more than a springboard into becoming a devotee (or "sannyasin") of his.

In 1981, Bhagwan moved to the United States, eventually settling on a huge tract of land in Oregon, soon to be known as Rajneeshpuram. There, his devotees worked eighty-hour weeks, sometimes paying for the privilege of so doing, bulldozing the land (and their remaining integrity) into submission, putting up buildings and putting down false roots, all under the blatantly neurotic eye of Bhagwan's secretary, Sheela. Though she was clearly a hostile, severely egocentric person, devotees submitted to her like sheep to a shepherd, gleefully making a virtue out of their non-resistance, forcing themselves to appear content, making being in physical proximity to Bhagwan more important than being authentic.

Bhagwan's face lost its balance and luminosity, his eyes lost their timelessness and depth, his discourses (when he began them again) lost their fire, originality, and grace, and his creation of Rajneeshism lost him all those who had loved him for his once eloquent disregard for all "ism's." An absurd number of Rolls-Royces were bought for him (yet another "device," of course!), armed guards appeared, paranoia accelerated, work became known as "worship," Sheela became even more arrogantly fascist, devotees buried themselves in gross denial, and Bhagwan, looking more and more drugged, appeared to be oblivious to it all. Rajneeshpuram had become but a concentration camp built and run by its inmates, now but a docile herd of idolatrous idiots and phony holies, working their butts (and but's!) off in order to ignore or deaden themselves to the brazen violations of human rights going on all around them, ever propagandizing each other with the assumption that they were participating in a "Buddhafield" (a psychophysical setting wherein the awakening process is quickened, or magnified). Bhagwan started making a smug fool of himself with the media, having reduced himself to an embarrassingly inarticulate parody of the man he had once been. Finally, Rajneeshpuram died a messy, unconscious death, suffocating in its own exhaust. Sheela went to jail, Bhagwan left the United States, and his devotees wandered about in a stupor, desperately avoiding disillusionment, doing whatever they could to prevent themselves from seeing their part in the abuses at Rajneeshpuram.

Eventually, Bhagwan returned to Poona, reestablishing himself there. Gushing with greying gratitude and amnesiac enthusiasm, his devotees fled back to Poona, blinding themselves to Bhagwan's actual condition, which was even worse than at Rajneeshpuram. He was now (and still is) less than a pale imitation of what he once was, lamely regurgitating the same old bullshit, and spicing it with enough irrelevant jokes to keep his herd entertained and fast, fast asleep — it is as if he is but a mouthpiece for their lowest possibilities, a medium reflecting back to them not their craving to be consoled and filled, but rather the verbal satisfaction of that craving. Yes, what a Master says is not a reflection of him, but of those around him, yet a real Master is no passive medium for the grossness and slumbering appetites personified all around him — instead, he is a pure medium for (and conscious embodiment of) the Source Itself, spontaneously committed to awakening those who come to him, rather than merely committed to satisfying their unillumined appetites. Long ago, Bhagwan was very close to being such a man. He is not now; he's simply going through the motions of being the object of guru-worship, seemingly unaware that he's attracting only the most lost of people, whereas he once, many years before, attracted more than a few intelligent, relatively balanced people, because he was then a man of integrity, a genius of synthesis, a magician of awakening's alchemy.

So how did he manage to lose it? Let us say that there were some dormant seeds in him, seeds whose presence he never acknowledged, even when they at last sprouted in America. He took far too much on, spreading himself too thin, again and again failing to *really* lay it on the line with his devotees — he was too busy praising them for being with him to give them the direct benefit of his undiluted criticism of them. Bhagwan lost his enlightenment because he never truly "had" it, except in a bodiless sort of way; he never really embodied his enlightenment, letting it permeate right to where his dormant seeds lay waiting. He fled his *full* humanness, and it eventually caught up with him, demanding his unqualified attention, but he only continued *acting* like a Master, instead of openly confessing his true inner whereabouts, which of course suited his devotees' desperate desire that he keep playing Master...

Most other guru-figures are not originals like Bhagwan Shree Rajneesh once was, but are only fronts for what they were taught by their guru, or through their lineage. Some of these are authentic teachers, but very few of them clearly address the pitfalls of being a devotee, especially if their path includes or necessitates devotion to the teacher. So how to tell the real from the false? First of all, be able to distinguish the real from the false in yourself. The key is not to look for signs or supposedly tell-tale evidence of authenticity or legitimacy, but to have center, to be *already* established, at least to some substantial degree, in one's native integrity of being; otherwise, one will be only succumbing to authority, be it the guru's, the guru-expert's, or just one's own internalized recoil from Daddy. Criteria presented for the recognition of a true guru or spiritual Master are usually little more than the arguments of do-gooder intellectualism, spewing out a logic (either of square-shouldered reactivity or of antiseptic erudition) that neatly fits into, and reinforces, our cultural addiction to simplistic how-to articles, lifestyle paint-by-numbers, and the ubiquitous ten easy steps to everything under the sun. Information is not enough — one must also be stably aligned with one's capacity and need for transformation, or one will mistake facts for the Truth...

In the realm of guru-recognition, no one wants to be fooled, or, better yet, exposed as a fool or sucker, so there is a suspicion of guru-figures, other than, of course, one's own; nevertheless, just about everyone participates daily in guru-worship in a generalized sense, be it of a person, a belief-system, a product, a goal, an institution, an organization, or whatever authoritative or parental entity makes them, or promises to make them, feel better, or more fulfillingly stimulated and cradled, especially if such feeling (which is only pumped-up sensation) gives them a sense of belonging to something grander than what they take themselves to be, something that roots them into its vast soil, something that sucks them into its bubble, something, in other words, that is cultic...

Almost anything can be a cult — Rajneeshism, television-evangelism, Werner Erhard's est, Muktananda's Siddha Yoga, Catholicism, Republicanism, minority rights, religion, psychiatry, drug-realities, fandom, marriage, and on and on — all it need do to qualify is to be self-enclosed, self-obsessed, opposed to its own transformation, and convinced that it is right. Any opposition from within is usually dismissed as "negativity," "resistance," "ungodliness," "ego," "blasphemy," "not getting it," or "sin," and therefore is taken as just cause for ostracization, excommunication, and even violence. Thus does a cult, by keeping only the true believers (even if there are only two, as in marriage), perpetuate itself and petrify its form. And do not forget the cult of "deprogramming" those who are in groups that are commonly viewed as cults; deprogrammers, stinking of diseased morality, are themselves unknowingly programmed, being no more than cleancut missionaries for their own beliefs. Guru-worship itself is a swooning soup of spiritually ambitious egos (ego being a cult of one), a broth of enthusiastic gullibility, a garishly obvious demonstration of cultism.

Cults are like seed-cases; initially, they protect what is inside, but soon, if they don't break or become permeable to their environment, they become the jailers for what is within, so that it merely rots, ossifies, or dies. However, even if it dies, its devotees keep worshipping it, ever retaining their status as fans of it, or of its successor. It is no accident that the word "fan" comes from the word "fanatic" — fandom, be it of rock musicians, movie stars, or guru-figures, is simply the socially acceptable side of the obsessive attachment central to fanaticism.

Fanatics are peculiarly attractive to those who are both unattached and without center; their very plantedness, their single-pointedness, their seeming absence of doubt, their unswerving commitment to the object of their fanaticism, gives them an aura of solidity, of familial steadiness and groundedness, that is very, very alluring to the uprooted, the homeless, the alienated, the disaffected, the searching, the lonely. Come join us, exude the fanatics, be they a political movement, a religious group, or a psychotherapeutic movement. Yes, come join us, come be part of our family, come take root with us, come steady your wandering soul, come realize your deepest goals with us, come help us combat the madness in our beloved land, come empower yourself to get that you've got it, come partake of the bliss of the Guru's Grace, come! Come join us, come live in the light, come heal yourself, come drink from the wisdom of the only Sadguru on the planet, come wash away your sins, come accept Jesus, come surround yourself with white light, come stand on your head, come affirm your magnificence and help usher in the New Age, come, come send in your donations, come enjoy prosperity consciousness, come! Come join us, come sit with a living Master, come chant for world peace, come help us restore order, come help us get rid of negativity, come help us keep our country white, come find yourself, come realize ultimate self-transcendence, come let's do it together, come let's spread the word, come!

And come see what's being spread. See all of this, shovelled high and wide, reeking of righteousness, steaming with perfumed rot and run-away thought, load after load of recycled excrement serving as religious cement, shitpiles of lunatic reasonableness, oozing from left and right, inside and outside, up and down, round and round, with numbing regularity, devotees and other fanatics sprouting up like mushrooms from all the bullshit, mushrooms with fat little heads and truth unsaid, each one a little jargonized sanctuary of poison, a little uprightness of false food and parasitic stature, giving all mushrooms a bad name...

Now let us take another guru-figure, one who has consistently demonstrated both originality and integrity. Da Free John (also known as Da Love-Ananda, with all sorts of additional appellations) is a lucid wonder of a man, effortlessly radiant, overflowing with sublime intelligence and heartfelt wisdom, teaching through his example the transcendence of all reactivity. Nevertheless, he sits at the center of a hive abuzz with rabid earnestness, misguided loyalty, and fetishistic preoccupation with him and his every move. He has eloquently criticized such foolishness again and again over the years, but to little avail; his devotees are far too busy telling themselves how wonderful he is, and how wonderful it is to have a Master like him, to really face their cultic obsession with him.

Like those around Bhagwan Shree Rajneesh, they glibly mind-fuck, ever painting themselves into a devotional corner, except they're more verbose, more emotionally constipated, and more rigidly "nice," drearily burdening themselves with their "good student" parrotings of Da Free John's teachings and manner of speech. They compulsively and almost constantly express, or intend to express, their gratitude for him with incredibly naive sincerity and disgusting adulation, robotically convincing themselves that they are doing the right thing, rarely noticing that they're just making real estate out of a moment of light. Like the devotees of other gurus, they chronically and unknowingly generate in themselves the very sensations, gross and subtle, that seem to them to be incontrovertible evidence that they *really* are in touch with their Guru, and they render their make-believe all the more real by using their imagination (and craving to fit in) to stir up the "right" emotions. The fact that this self-deception is occasionally punctuated by moments of real communion with Da Free John only strengthens the lie that they are living.

In their supposed yielding to the Divine, to the Transcendental Reality (as personified by Da Free John), they are keeping a lookout for signs of spiritual maturation, not knowing that they are doing little more than building ladders for their ego. Da Free John obviously sees this, for he has addressed it many times, and criticized it with great force, but he has not said an uncompromising no to it, a no backed by firm and specific consequences. He might claim that he is giving his devotees room to fuck up, time and space to evolve beyond their obsession with him, but he has not really taken a *solid* stand, except verbally, against such neurotic fixation, because to do so would necessarily mean an end to their guru-worshipping (or their departure from his organization), and he has made such devotionalism the very foundation of his way, again and again stressing the primacy of devotion to the Guru, arguing its necessity with compelling passion, subtlety, and logic, proclaiming in so many words that, in order to replicate his condition, to stand where he stands relative to the Divine Reality, a devotional relationship to him is essential.

And why are his devotees so obsessed with replicating his condition? Is it because they want to fully awaken? Is it because they want to be in a state of unqualified oneness with God? No! It is because they sense such replication as a shortcut, an *escape* from the demands of their own individuality, which they've, to a significant degree, denied and avoided in order to fit themselves to the path he's outlined for them. And why should they have to awaken through the means that worked for him? Only because they have convinced themselves that there is no other way for them. Thus do they turn away from the uniqueness of their own being, denying expression to whatever in them does not conform to the path they're glued to, fleeing the very qualities of self that must be faced for there to be true integration, wholeness of being, and center. They don't seem to realize, except intellectually, that enlightenment is of the *entire* being, including every darkness, hurt, trauma, and idiosyncracy of body and mind, even though Da Free John has told them so (albeit with excessive abstraction) — they avoid directly feeling this realization and its imperatives, because they don't want, except in contrived moments of "consideration," to nakedly face, feel, and penetrate the very motive that keeps them stuck being mere devotees around Da Free John, penned up in their minds like so many articulate cattle.

The point here is not to dismiss or abandon beings like Da Free John, but to make good use of them. Standing apart from them like suspicious, emotionally insulated adolescents or scientists is just as foolish as playing devotee to them. Before we consider a saner approach, let us ask why Da Free John permits and encourages the whole drama of guru and devotee. How can he do so, given his undeniable intelligence and remarkable clarity of insight into the human condition? The meat of the answer has to do with the fact that frozen parent-child conflicts must be thawed before spiritual maturity is possible, and devotionalism, through its sheer heat (and infantile craving for unity through identification with an all-pervading parent), exaggerates such conflicts to such a degree that they are clearly exposed, ripe to be passed through.

Unfortunately, Da Free John doesn't use devotionalism in this light, but rather encourages its continuation far past the point where it ought to have served its purpose, instead of employing it as a psychotherapeutic purification. He denounces cultism, yet tacitly supports it, letting himself be surrounded by ritualized guru-worship, apparently not seeing that such perversion of emotion, such excess of "positive" feeling, is but the flip side of the excessive intellectuality of his movement. His devotees are instructed to "consider" the fully enlightened condition in the midst of whatever they are up to — at best, this illuminates their current circumstance, reminding them that God is already the case, rather than a goal. More often than not, however, this "considering" only goes to mind, taking root there as one more burdensome "should." Of course, it is up to devotees what they do with this, but what about Da Free John's responsibility? Why does he insist on what so, so easily degenerates into mere mind-fucking? Why doesn't he have his devotees create a solid, down-to-earth foundation before the walls go up? He has done this through their organization, but not *within* each devotee, except superficially, because to really do so, to build true center, one cannot just be a devotee — one must become a full individual, capable both of standing one's own unique ground, and of living in unrestrained resonance with the Source of All.

Da Free John seems to associate individuality with neurotic independence; he continually talks about the non-existence of separate beings, the illusion of separateness and of individuated self. Yes, such non-existence is literally true at certain levels of being, and is utterly obvious in the enlightened or near-enlightened condition, but not at the level inhabited by guru-worshippers. Their transparency, their sense of oneness, or non-separateness, with the Divine is but romantic delusion, created not by an expansion of their personal boundaries, but by an irresponsible dissolution of them. They have but fled form and mortality, seeking refuge in devotionalism's infantile bubble.

Like just about everyone else, guru-worshippers still need to explore their egos, their quirks, their patterns, their turn-on's and turn-off's, without automatically seeing them as obstacles to spiritual growth, or as illusions. Their work is to go with open eyes into and through everything that seems to be them, with such passion, commitment, and loving attention that they outgrow their need to be somebody special (including being a devotee of the Greatest Master of all), and thus begin to become true individuals, simultaneously solid and transparent, firmly yet flexibly rooted in their center of being, no longer trying to escape from their "limitations." Such is the ground from which real transformation can occur; devotionalism is but part of its fertilizer, existing only to be fermented beyond itself...

Da Free John has let himself become a cultic object, except perhaps to some of those who are most personally intimate with him. Nevertheless, he has not, like Bhagwan Shree Rajneesh, slipped into a parody of himself — he is still a man of brilliant insight and creative genius. So why does he let himself be personified as the Divine Reality, and worshipped as such? His oneness with God is fundamentally no different than anyone else's, except that it is far more obvious. As he has said, there is only God, forever appearing as all of this. And if there is only God, why turn away from any of it, including one's own ego? Why malign the ego, robotically labelling it Narcissus, as his devotees drearily do? Why dissociate from ego, when such dissociation is but the escapist side of egocentricity? Why not participate in and enjoy the show, the whole show, and get on with it? Why such obsession with transcendence? What is there to escape from? Transcendence is not escape, except to those who would flee or deny their own unique being, bleating that the only true being is that of the Guru...

The one way, the one Truth, the one God, the one deodorizer, the one team, the one channel, the one answer, the one One, the one! Such a mad cloister of one's, such a frenzy of certainty, such a ubiquitous caricature of real unity! And, at the same time, such a deep hunger, such a need, such a longing, such an undying longing for union with God, a longing doomed to fail so long as it is kept in the dark, or on a devotional leash, making a bound and gagged appearance in the ego's "spiritual" service.

To make wise use of someone like Da Free John, whatever his failings, we must not submit to devotional fervour, nor simply stand back, taking notes. We must feel him, empathize with him, receive him, give to him, losing face without losing touch, giving our love without giving ourselves away. We must remain centered yet not impermeable, strong in our very vulnerability, and then we can, if appropriate, even dissolve into the transcendent condition without any separating-out from the stuff of Life, without any sidestepping of emotion, dark or light.

Then escape is no longer an option — the call to awaken is no longer an invitation, but a demand, an irresistible imperative. Then there is no fixation of attention on a man like Da Free John, but rather only sane regard, whether appreciative, critical, or both. Then guru-worship is but a memory, an obsolete strategy, no more than a souvenir of diseased childhood.

The fruits of excessive or badly-handled dependence during childhood are either a continuation of such dependence, as in the guru-worshipper, or a retreat into perpetual adolescence and deified independence, as in the guru-condemner, or an obsessive clinging to the superficial, as in the phony tolerance of liberalism and "New Age" thinking. All three are solutions to what ought to have never been a problem in the first place — the profound helplessness and dependence of infancy and early childhood.

Very few parents have worked through their own neurotic reactions to their early years to such an extent that they can sanely parent themselves, let alone their children; all too often, they only unknowingly transmit their own diseased past, making their children pay the price for their own failure to live from their core, again and again demanding loyalty to "their" ethics, or else making a virtue out of their permissiveness, leaving the ground between "yes" and "no" vague and muddy. How can they possibly teach true discipline when they have next to none themselves? And how can they truly nurture, when they themselves are so, so undernourished inside, so, so starving for authenticity?

And how can they teach Truth, when they are living a lie? And how can they teach freedom and responsibility, which ought to go hand in hand, level upon level, when they themselves inhabit a self-made trap that they only long to replace with a cosier trap, one that is but one huge entertainment center, crammed with round-the-clock distractions? Their obsession with being constantly occupied with something, inner or outer, anything to keep them from facing their depths (and what they did to themselves in order to survive *their* parents), drives them, in well-intentioned mechanicalness, to keep their children occupied, over-stimulated, over-exposed to quick hits of sensation, and thus all but out of reach of inner stillness, meditativeness, and true alertness, not to mention sensitivity, ecstasy, and heartfelt responsibility. For such children, discipline is a burden, an interruption of "play," little more than a means to snare parental or teacherly approval. Their capacity for center is all but destroyed through the rigidly ordered chaos of their world, making them prime candidates for guru-worship and cultism, utterly marooned from any real sanity of spirit, desensitized to Truth, repetitiously mistaking the dominant fragment of their fractured self as the real them...

Some adults recognize the trap, and a rare few do something about it, something more than whining about angst and programming and victimization. These few, no matter how atrocious their childhood was, don't use it as an alibi for now, nor do they leave its difficulties unresolved — they cultivate center, no matter how painful the purification required of them. They love with open eyes. They have guts. Their surrender to the awakening process deepens their individuality. They are no longer suffering a case of mistaken identity. They have not yet fully arrived, but are definitely on their way. Though guru-worship is not an option for them, they do not necessarily avoid guru-figures, often finding immense value in having some association with such beings...

33

Parenting,
Freedom, And Responsibility

Parents who are without center cannot help but participate in child-abuse, however well-intentioned they are — they can't even sanely and lovingly parent *themselves*, let alone their children. With blind insistence, they transmit their disease of being, their unresolved anger, hurt, frustration, helplessness, and falseness, invading their children over and over again with their neurotic programs for survival, compulsively associating the inculcation of such gross misalignment with true guidance. They literally force their children to act a role other than their real selves, because they themselves are doing *exactly* the same thing, with barely any awareness that they are suffering a severe case of mistaken identity. Instead of being a parent, they *act* like a parent, mechanically obeying a script they never wrote.

No matter how good-hearted they might be, no matter how benign their approach, they inevitably do harm to their children, simply because they are asleep to (or turned away from) their own depths, asleep to the fullness of their being, and therefore also to their children's — even their love, at its best, is little more than misguided comfort or over-protective support, a kind of intoxicating applause for a fine *acting* job, an all-encompassing, generous warmth and affection that is subliminally riddled with the admonition to never *truly* leave, to always, wherever one is, stay tucked in with Mommy and Daddy, to, in other words, never truly grow up, never authentically wean oneself from one's parents, except superficially. Thus is diseased childhood (and its reactive opposite, diseased adolescence) propagated, overwhelming all but the most peripheral pruning (social programs, psychoanalysis, counselling, conventional meditation), forming the very foundation of a culture obsessed with infantile cravings, parental approval, and emotional anaesthetization, a culture perpetually at war with itself, finding peace only in the oblivion of pleasurable stimulation and sedation...

Few parents understand freedom, since they are so used to living an imprisoned existence, having thoroughly embodied their entrapping assumptions about Life and themselves. Even fewer understand the relationship between freedom and responsibility, because they've made themselves all but incapable of both, reducing freedom to licence, and responsibility to a "should"-infested, joyless duty.

Freedom is not an option for those who are without center, for they are almost always bound, however spacious their surroundings, held prisoner by their very suppression of being, their so-called freedoms little more than the chronic bingeing of drunk slaves. They are deafened by their round-the-clock snore, mistaking the arguments of their conditioning for Truth's roar, thinking that freedom's just an exaggerated kind of permission, a right that can be exercised by *anyone*. Christ could be standing in front of them, or their ideal sexual partner, or their Big Moment, and they would still remain committed to their robotic destiny, unable to make wise use of such an opportunity — their very structuring of themselves, their unwillingness to truly parent themselves, their failure to love, would make them *impermeable* to the fullness of such events or influences, capable only of reactivity. Christ would all too soon be crucified, ignored, or turned into a cultic object, reduced to fodder for evangelical fanaticism and "Christian" ideology; the ideal sexual partner would rapidly become a pornographic beacon for masturbatory fantasy (especially that of romance), a juicy place to fuck away stress, a fine place to get a load off one's mind, a combination super stimulant and super sleeping pill; the Big Moment would quickly pass without having been deeply felt, soon becoming a favourite object for nostalgic regurgitation, a topic to haul out during the mediocre recitations known as social conversation.

Freedom is independent of circumstances, inner and outer. It is the very essence of being at home with the totality of oneself. It is a choice only for those who are capable of *real* choice, those who are permitting the fire of the awakening process to do its work. Freedom is what happens when we naturally and whole-heartedly embrace the fullness of our being, and when we have also developed a corresponding capacity for responsibility at the level at which our freedom is occurring — we must, in other words, be responsible for maintaining the environment, inner and outer, that best supports our *current* degree of freedom. When we are capable of an increase in responsibility, we need to take it on (or be guided into doing so by our parents, if we are not yet adults), or we'll stagnate, having deprived ourselves of a corresponding increase in freedom. This is not about rising to one's level of incompetence, as in the Peter Principle, but is about skilfully playing the edge of one's functional competency, with both sensitivity and guts.

Freedom needs the ground of real responsibility; otherwise, its flights will be but escapes, forever parachuting down into trouble. Freedom is an unfolding, not a given. Children need to learn, and learn with their whole beings, the relationship between freedom and responsibility at *every* stage of their growth. If they are denied the opportunity of a particular responsibility at a time when they are ripe for it, they will almost invariably make a *problem* out of such responsibility later in life, enslaving themselves to it or rebelling against it, thus making themselves inaccessible to its accompanying freedom.

For example, very young children, even infants, are quite capable of being sensitive to those around them; if such sensitivity is not required of them when they are clearly capable of giving it (and this requirement or "demand" is *not* just purely verbal direction, but rather is profoundly artful, body-oriented guidance and example, delivered with love, ease, appropriate intensity, and right timing), they will only continue their self-obsession, especially if it's seen as cute or "natural," thereby carrying what was pure need in their infancy forward into manipulative, loveless, insensitive "need" in their childhood and adolescence. Teaching children sensitivity to others at the right time is a great gift to them — it expands their world, while keeping their heart empathetically open. Such children play with exuberance, but can easily also play quietly when there is a need for a low noise level in their household. Such children do not crawl all over their parents, whining for attention; in fact, they do not whine at all, for in their very sensitivity to others, and vice versa, they feel already included, already loved, already at ease with themselves.

What I have described cannot be taught by parents who are not living an open-hearted, grounded life, a life rich with center and integrity. The relationship between freedom and responsibility cannot be taught mechanically. It cannot be forced on children — it is a transmission of knowingness, a largely non-verbal transfer of innate wisdom, a gift that must move if parenting is to be authentic, a gift that is already there to be given...

34

Marriage, Entrapment, & The True Woman

Marriage is usually no more than a parody of intimacy, a socially sanctified pact to play it safe and deadly secure, to make a lifestyle out of mutually enmeshed superficiality, cowardice, hypocrisy, robotic consistency, sexual aberration, and unrelenting anaesthetization of the awakening impulse, the whole damned ego-consoling charade of it all oozing mechanical sincerity, snoozing and cruising up and down the hotline paved between brain and crotch, hoping for the best and dying in the nest, ever dressed to kill real love, ever injecting itself with cosy little delusions of commitment, fidelity, and joy, not seeing that its very obsession with not making security-upsetting waves (not to mention the tsunami of awakening!) has all but reduced it to a cement boat upon a cement sea with no sky except that of romantic fantasy.

Even in most of those rare marriages where there is some heartfelt integrity and some degree of wakefulness, emotional sterility and spiritual staleness eventually take root, dulling the couple's edge, level upon level, gradually eroding their bond, no matter how strenuously they try to compensate with various stimulation-strategies and tactile tactics, no matter how thorough their efforts to keep resurrecting their passion and love, no matter how ardently they try to change the system, namely their marriage, from within — sooner or later, they settle for less than fullness from each other, making a virtue out of their deadening compromise, righteously rationalizing it, not *deeply* questioning the actual structure of their marriage itself, going on and on, resolutely making the best of their self-entrapment, rather than creating a more life-giving arrangement, all the while knowing they are in a bind, yet repetitiously reinforcing it through their clinging to the very consolations, sexual and otherwise, that they find within their marriage, again and again settling for a half-hearted intimacy, assuming that this is the way it has to be...

Those jokes that snickeringly imply that marriage is, for men, the beginning of a long downslide, a tying-down, an inevitable and bizarrely honourable drafting into a henpecked army, are accurate in their theme of entrapment, but not in their portrayal of women as the captors, or victors. Marriage, in the case of men, may seem to be the end of freedom, packed with resignation, stupidly smiling good cheer, force-fed monogamy, and the applause of others in a similar bind, but the apparent freedom that preceded marriage was not freedom at all, but only an irresponsible running around inside a cage of promiscuous opportunity. Getting married after such "freedom" is just a putting down of plastic roots in another sort of cage, accompanied by a largely unacknowledged internalizing of promiscuous proclivity — such intent is usually buttoned-up with a facade of respectability and sexual fidelity, a facade whose flag is enthusiastically waved by the just-married, and feebly saluted by the inmates of long-term marriage, those stalwarts who have dutifully resigned themselves to their impotence, growing old without growing wise, slowly rotting inside their jockstraps, ever comforting themselves with misguided notions of loyalty...

And what of women? They also tend to betray themselves in marriage, often having a clearer sense of what is happening than their husbands, but usually do little more about it than chronically complain, all the while making a sterile virtue out of their being married, as though it were some kind of *achievement*. They make their apparent security more important than their integrity, spreading their legs in joyless duty or in a pleasure-seeking heat tainted by make-believe love. Whether they houseclean the cage, or are salary slaves, or are entrepreneurs, they are just as trapped as their husbands, despite their slightly superior knowledge of their circumstances.

Even if women flee into the arms of feminism, they are still trapped, for feminism is just a more sophisticated kind of cultism (marriage being a cult of two), gagging on its own ideology, blaming men for all kinds of ills, but not really seeing the crucial role women play in many of the very same ills. Feminism does not give women their voice, but only *its* voice, its emotional aridity, its depersonalized, spiritually-vacant stridency and righteousness, thereby arming women not with passion for the awakening process, but only with egoic consolation, narcissistic logic, and a "sisterhood" that has more to do with psychological fascism than with love. Feminism is little more than patriarchy in drag, obsessed by its own bleating; it is invulnerable, hard, angular, and terrified of real womanliness, making the same neurotic association as most men do between dependency and helplessness, thereby setting in motion the deification of independence, or perpetual adolescence, that now plagues the Earth with its self-centered, runaway consumerism and craving for pleasurable distraction.

The true woman yields neither to conventional marriage, nor to feminism, nor to any other "ism," but only again and again renews her commitment to cultivating true center, without any avoidance of intimacy (including that recoil from intimacy known as "spiritual" renunciation). She loves women and she loves men, and her love is not ideological, nor nice, but is nakedly obvious, powerful in its sensitivity and vulnerability. Her security is not in cultic association with anything (or anyone), including marriage, feminism, and the "freedoms" of neurotic independence, but rather is in her unqualified embracing of the *inherent* insecurity of Life. She takes risks not to prove something, but as a celebration of being alive, an intensification of love, an open-eyed leap into the Unknown and the Unknowable. If she is married, she is not a wife, but an adventuress, a warrior, an oracle, a lover, a truth-speaker, an earthy flowering, a brilliance.

If she is a mother, she treats her children not as mere extensions of herself, nor as dolls, nor as security blankets, nor as pride-producers, nor does she let them be indoctrinated by stultifying beliefs and societal taboos — her children do not whine, but shine with joy, not the joy that comes from getting some candy or some sort of privilege, but the joy that comes from being sensitive to Life, so sensitive (and simultaneously relaxed) that exaggerated or instant stimulation is not needed in order to feel good, as is the case with all too many children. There is no dullness, sourness, resignation, or spiritlessness in the eyes of a true woman's children; even in their infancy, she has, through skilful and ever-spontaneous means, again and again helped them to reestablish themselves in pure feeling, or unrestrained communion with the forces that govern Life. She is bonded with her children, but not in bondage with them, having gracefully guided herself and them through weaning after weaning, without any diminishment in intimacy.

Back to marriage — it is essential to see what humans have actually made of marriage, even if it upsets our entire life, unmistakably necessitating not just change or rearrangement of our circumstances and inner life, but actual transformation. Marriage is almost always no more than a self-enclosed little bubble of false independence, tidily equipped with its own little possessions, name, and cultic rituals, functioning as a gross parody of real family, mechanically making a pioneer-like virtue out of its isolation (which it obscures by assuming a kinship with other families living in similar fashion). However, such families do not live, but only survive, cloning their children from their own automaticities, periodically complaining about the mess the world's in, not seeing that they are but part of the problem.

What our culture calls "family" makes authentic community impossible, for such community requires not a conglomerate of little marriage-centered families, but family itself, true family, bound not by vows, nor by common belief, nor by force-fed "commitment," but by firmly established intimacy and mutual commitment to being a sanctuary for the establishment of full humanness, whatever the cost. This, of course, necessitates firmly established center in leaders, and, more importantly, some degree of center in everyone involved, a quality and steadiness of center that only begins when one's neurotic attachment to one's past is undone. To even begin to consider such an undertaking is a step very few are willing to take, a step into a radical re-evaluation of everything in one's culture and one's life, a step that cries to be begun...

35

Birthing The Man

(the gong is struck
the song begun, pulsing with muscular waves
surging rough & tender, shimmering with thunderous grace
weeping and roaring for manhood's true face)

Some men, recoiling from hardness, are stuck in softness, fearing and forgetting their buried violence, hiding in gutless tenderness, sucking their soft-shelled carapace ever inward, ever tighter, squeezing out impotent tears, squeezing the power from their breath, compulsively gathering consoling jargon for their rigid stand against the exercise of undiluted force, again and again trying to trade their balls for guaranteed mothering, literally caving in to prove their assertion of harmlessness.

How easily they make raw male power wrong! How easily they smudge and scorn its lyrics! How readily they associate it with mere savagery! And how eager they are to please their babyhood's mother, to become more and more sophisticated beggars for her multi-headed applause!

In the vacuum left by their fathers, the back-slapping absence, the dutiful hollow, the heavy-handed desolation, the clumsy separation, the cement swirl of misguided challenge and mishandled nurturance, the unquestioned failures of nerve, the taboo of unsentimental tenderness, the extinction of full-hearted manly touch, in that vacuum, that dream-framed vacuum, that emptiness battle-numbed and so goddamned reasonably resigned, such men ricochet like thoughts in an unawakened mind, bouncing between stern shoulds, blindly castrating their integrity, their passion, their force, efficiently bottling the pain, sterilizing the screams, and bottling the rest, leaving it in neatly labelled display in the museum of their gelded remains.

Fleeing their full maleness, they dwell in offices of mind, worldly or other-worldly, greening their deserts of abstraction and spirit-contraction with oases of push-button flesh, desperately fucking mirages of Mommy, male or female, ever feeling guilty for being male, repeatedly sacrificing their anorexic warrior on cleancut altars, offering his heart and belly to their deified fear while they march for peace, secretly designing and refining new weapons for their inner war, crushing their impulse to pass through a saner door.

(the gong resounds
loosening a male music, a sinewed joy,
a daring leap full of shining boy,
a jump power-sure into fully human heartland)

Other men, hiding in the foxholes of their maleness, vacate their vulnerability, unquestioningly paving the wasteland of their anaesthetized torso, keeping a hot-line open between brain and groin, a pornographic dialogue of scantily-clad taboos and quick-rushing heat, their chest but a no-man's-land, a rotting fortress, their belly, flat or bloated, a meatiness of misaligned power, their jaw and loins obsessed with thrust, with getting ahead, their flesh burdened by decades of split-level lust.

Making adult sounds as they race up and down the freeways of diseased boyhood, they allow their warrior to be exploited, to be reduced to little more than a fighting and fucking machine, a robotic doer impaled on patriotic consistency, a square-shouldered puppet of invulnerable shoulds, a blustering pawn of rapist impulse and slumber-management.

How easily such men rationalize self-mutilation, calling it duty! How easily they plaster stimulation-pinups on their spiritual oblivion! How readily they turn away from the enemy's child, even as they turn away from their own softness, their own innocence, running and running from the boy inside them, the broken boy loitering in a toughened loneliness, emptied of himself, already hardened for the next command, steeling himself against feeling, against revealing, against magic, thinking and shrinking himself into a logic of heartless survival and maximization of pleasurable distraction, grimly defending the boundaries of his false self, trusting only his mistrust.

(again the gong strikes
pouring out its thought-free shout, its fluid boom
the sleeper blinks in the trembling rectangle of his dream,

flirting with elusive meaning;
faraway he can almost hear someone screaming)

Yet the arms of all men, however armoured, insensitive, calculating, or committed to building mansions for their pride, carry a shade of reaching, a reaching perhaps embarrassing to their minds, a reaching straining with subterranean quivers of heart, whether encrusted by neediness, as in the neurotically soft man, or by roughness and gruffness, as in the exaggeratedly hard man, or by seductive slickness, as in the obsessively tailored man — it is a reaching rooted in both warrior and child, man and boy, outgoing and ingoing, thrust and welcome, a reaching of and for love, a love that does not have to be bought or earned, but only lived, a love vibrant with rejuvenative risk and adventure, a love aflame with awakening's alchemy...

Men and men and men, fighting their reaching, so busy being the battleground for their inner war, victor and vanquished sinking into bloody mud, crushed together flesh to flesh, cheek to cheek, fear to fear, heartache to heartache, yet still far apart, sinking and sinking, every woman a minefield, a choice hunk of real estate, a poisoned harbour, a red-carpet nightmare, a voluptuous suction, a dreamy promise, a hideout, a cultic sanctuary, a womb and a tomb, forever unescapable, even by those who, fleeing the call of their flesh, chant, pray, meditate, fast, and concentrate upwards in the luminous cave behind their forehead, seeking immunity in the stillpoint's infinite bubble, struggling to somehow permanently abide in the formless dimension of God, thus separating themselves from the sacred demands of their humanness, ever finding themselves re-embodied by their very avoidance of true manliness, which is also avoidance of the Female, whether personal or archetypal.

Men and men and men! Some, successful enough to recognize and *feel* their failure, stop playing buddy to their armour, hard or soft...

(the rippling pound and tremor of the gong
its deep-rhythmed waves shaping a truer ground,
releasing love, grief, and unmutilated rage,
clearing some space in every gripped ribcage)

A few men, gutsy enough to unpeel and reveal, without gelding or ossifying their power, find a boy crouched in their dark, the long, long dark, the orphaned, arid dark, a sobbing boy, a boy crushed and bleeding, hammering and hammering against the inside of their chest, hammering and hammering with tiny fists, a boy bruised and divided, shoulders sagging, throat and Truth far apart, a weeping boy with not enough father and too much mother, already either enemy or slave to the Feminine, just like Daddy, but still nevertheless hammering and hammering, screaming to be felt, to be touched, to be known, to be held, to be initiated into the truly Masculine, screaming and scream- ing, squashed by grownup silence, betrayed by robotic associations between vulnerability and weakness, or between vulnerability and the acquisition of wraparound mothering, betrayed and betrayed, betrayed left and right, day and night, hard and soft, wimp and macho, liberal and conservative, betrayed and betrayed...

And still the boy calls, however indirectly, calling and calling for love, for the jailor's love, for the man's love, for love, goddamn it, love plain and simple, love uncluttered by mind, love pure and direct and god- damn the paternal patter, the embarrassed impotence, the turning away, the slamming doors and empty-hearted explanations, the fake eyes, the fucking resignation, the sagging duty! Goddamn the plastic sky, no more than the ceiling of Daddy's hungriest thought! And Goddamn the lame acceptance of that intolerable knot pulled so tight between sternum and spine! A weeping boy calling and calling, his eyes brimming with his smothered echo, his heart dropping between his ragged knees...

Men and men and men! Do you not see the machine-eyed conse- quences rising up amidst your ruins? The toxic flowers outlining your supposed name, dripping black, oozing with parasitic collusion and well-dressed confusion? Do you not sense the secondhand scent, the perfumed rot of romantic delusion, the advertised bleatings of superfi- cial release, the glorification of masturbatory titillation, the addiction to being consoled? Do you not feel the frozen or jellied jaw, the slitted or mind-fitted glance, the classroom whipping of up-start cries, the righteous cruelty, the flesh-branded disguise, the emotional hard-on? Or the haloed wimphood, the limping passion, the righteous flight from anger and lust, the New Age should, flashing a spiritual smile, proclaiming oneness while dividing everything into positive and negative?

Men and men and men! Do you not recognize the obsession with texture, be it hard or soft, rough or smooth, attractive or unattractive? The obsession with doing it right? The unhealed hurt festering beneath deodorized shitpiles of computerized mind? Do you not feel your compulsive urge for distraction from the roots of what's really troub- ling you? Do you not feel the clean-shaven mess, the fear to purely and fully confess what you are *actually* doing, and do you not feel the innocence you will not truly bless, the horror of pretending that Father knows best, the disease of pretending you're not pretending, the heartbreak that cries for more than a superficial mending?

> *(the gong finds a richer thunder,*
> *dissolving the narcotic grip of Time*
> *now the body no longer penned up in the mind*
> *now the heart streaming through the eyes)*

Men! Your father staggers blind drunk through a maze of foggy streets, archaic avenues, degraded alleys, nylon labyrinths, bloody ditches, cement canyons, smoky livingrooms, his paycheck crumpled in one hand, his despair in the other, his face a defeated fist or an optimistic list, his stride not his, his boyhood crushed behind his belief-riddled eyes, his pride muting his cries.

Men! Your father loiters in you, his muffled needs and curses and inculcated verses animating your daze, sculpting you, defining your stance, binding you to a rigid dance, driving you into your headquarters to wage needless wars; it is his chest, whether inflated or deflated, through which you all too easily wander and squander your juice, desperately searching for the treasure, the quick-buck or super-fuck grail, searching and searching, fighting false dragons, fucking false maidens, living in castles of surrogate maleness, resolutely seeding your sons with the same disease, the same goddamned soul-freeze.

Men! Must you do to your heart what your father did to you? Must you wear his shoes, or the opposite? Must you submit to, or spear him? Must you continue merely reacting to him? Only in truly standing apart from him, only in fully weaning yourself from his vision of you, only in intimacy with the authority native to yourself, only in claiming your own ground, only in the clarity and rejuvenative thrill of your own spirit-land, your own heart's primal demand, can you really forgive your father, and then you will not be apart from him, wherever he might be, dead or alive, receptive or shut — you will be neither child nor adolescent relative to him, or anyone or anything else.

Men and men and men! Your father wanders large but vague across a quivering snapshot held in place behind your eyes, and your mother fills the foreground, whether passively or actively, her eyes brimming with promised milk and sweet bedtimes, her touch, given or not, loving or dutiful, craved and craved, and her presence, dark or light, hard or soft, meek or domineering, made irresistible by an unmistakable aura of womb, of eternal sanctuary. And you linger at the bottom of the photograph, no larger than a thumbprint, sporting a half-frozen smile, your eyes belonging to two very different faces, your seedling grief but the faintest of smudges, your youth already sprouting parent-pleasing masks...

Your seedling grief, your knowingness of self-betrayal, now a forest in which you roam, lost and bound. Do you not hear your own cries? Do you mistake them for another's? Someone childish, someone you've of course long since outgrown?

(deeper into now
the gong's sound all around
filling out breath and blood
awakening the spirit of flesh)

Men and men and men! Listen to *your* cry, listen to its earth and sky! Listen to its hidden strength, its noble core, feel the music of its Everlasting door! Let your cry, your roar, your pure shout, run down through your legs and feet, its wild, muscular roots plunging into moist, quivering soil! Let your cry grow wings strong and wide, until your forehead is an infinity of sky, and your haunches gleam with exultation! Let your shout blast through the babbled clutter and mutter of your mentalizing! Let your cry be free, virginal, ashimmer with the unbridled fullness of you, the power and grace and pain and sweetness of quintessential maleness!

Men and men, and men! Give your inner listening a heart, letting the inside and outside be lovers, intertwined beneath starry covers! Give your passion an eye both sensitive and gutsy, both empathetic and lusty! Give your balls breathing room and glorious dignity! Give your manhood its true voice! Give Tarzan permission to weep, and give the woman in you your all, dying and exploding and birthing through your naked thrust, your luminous rocketing, your sweating grace and ecstatic loss of face...

Eat these lines, bite deep, bite fierce, bite orgasmically, crack all the pits, tonguing out the kernel and crushing it, absorbing its sudden nectar, its bittersweet depths, its sword and flower, knowing that it is to *your* release that you are being invited, rather than to just another remedial program. Brother, father, and son, child and elder, newborn and dying, poet and samurai, far and near, foggy and clear, all in one, I

hear you calling, calling and calling, calling through me, in me, for me,
as me, calling and calling, ever birthing the man.

> (the gong is still, but its sound rolls on
> guiding us, purifying our love and will
> until our everything's athrill
> a full-blooded silence sprouts within the murmurous boom
> and the Eternal Lover fleshes out the man,
> the warrior overflowing with joy,
> full of shining boy)

36

Myth
As Transformative Metaphor

Myths do not explain, but reveal. They are not meant to be analyzed, but felt. What symbols are to the mind, myths are to the heart.

Myths dramatize various archetypes of behaviour, using a language that is more akin to the dreaming state than to the so-called waking state. The storylines of myths may appear to be unnecessarily detailed in places, or even clogged with irrelevancies, but, like dreams, they are wonderfully efficient in the dynamics of their contents, gracefully multi-levelled, naturally subtle, painting an eloquent picture rather than describing it, ever inviting us to nakedly step through their quivering frames...

The trials and tribulations of a myth's protagonist reflect much more than egocentric struggle — the resemblance to a soap opera is only superficial, for where a soap opera exists only to profit from exploiting its viewers' fascination with their own subhuman compulsions, a myth simultaneously presents *and* illuminates such compulsions. Myths don't merely express what is neurotic or noble; they metaphorically expose the underpinnings of it. Myths clarify the human condition, when they are heard by more than the mind, but cultural melodrama, whether cinematic, literary, or everyday, only serves to reinforce the grossest aspects of the human condition, or to sentimentalize its finer moments. Where melodrama sedates and distracts, myth expands and enriches.

Myths are doorways into the Unknowable. We pass through such entrances not to accumulate anything whatsoever, but to realize our true condition, to uninhibitedly embody our true identity. Every real myth supports this journey of being, by broadening the picture, by melodically articulating the preparatory work, by filling out forgotten places in us, by contributing to our ripening. Implicit here is a well-developed, intuitive understanding of myth, an understanding not confined to one's mind, but sensed by the totality of one.

Myths are not about facts, but about Truth. They don't so much tell the Truth, as breathe it. At the same time that myths demystify human behaviour and aspiration, they sensitize us to Mystery Itself, the Mystery that is the Source and Substance of All, the Mystery that forever appears as all of this, inviting us to feel It so fully that we become It, even as our individuality flowers...

Myths are the dreams of the transpersonal; they are creations taking form at the threshold of awakening, eloquent shapings of sublime perception, offered to all of us, shared by every human, asking only for our undivided attention, our wakeful wonder, our pure participation.

Myths are psychic theatre, serving to personify the psychophysical nature of the Universe. Their stories are not intended to inform, but to transform. Those who take myths as only bits of colourful information, or as mere anecdotes, or only as fodder for analysis or scholarly dissection, have missed the point. Like dreams, myths say what must be said with a beautifully encapsulated economy of language and gesture. To hear, to really hear, their metaphoric message, one must be potently receptive, alertly available. One must be curious, and one must be genuinely interested in knowing oneself. Otherwise, myths are but melodramas, bits of entertainment, swallowed all too literally, treated just the way modern cultures treat their dreams: with minimal interest and minimal intelligence.

Unlike soap operas, myths don't reinforce psychological fragmentation, but teach connectedness. Myths always accompany human culture, in one form or another. Whether ancient or modern, Odysseus or Superman, Narcissus or Frankenstein, Krishna or Galactus, Beowulf or Darth Vader, the world of myth is a world we must inhabit, or else we will be less than ourselves, partial and impoverished, chained to our mind's version of what's what, cut off from our depths, imprisoned in labyrinths of concrete and silicon chips.

Become more sensitive to your guiding myths. Identify them. Feel them. Know them. Let them become allies. Let them undo your secret disguise. Let them teach you about grief and wonder. Go through them, with gratitude. Breathe them bright. Remember your dreams tonight. Remember that myths are more real than facts. Remember that in our culture myths are all but synonymous with lies (as in "Myth or Fact?" lists in various media outlets). Cut through this. Reestablish myth as transformative metaphor, taking care that meaning is not superimposed on experience, but emerges *from* it, when necessary. In other words, don't automatically look for meaning, but rather look inside your looking, letting your insights lose their mind, letting your everything come ever more alive...

37

The Seven Main Centers
Of Life-Energy

The centers described below are not self-enclosed entities — each is but the primary locus of a particular realm of experience. Their descriptions are not meant to rigidly classify, but rather to clarify. Although they are active in all of us, they only work together harmoniously in those who are consciously and consistently established in their center of being...

CENTER	FUNCTION	WAY OF WORKING	LOCATION	ELEMENTAL PARALLEL
Root	Stability, Attachment	Instinct, Crystallization	Perineum, Anus, Coccyx, Feet	Mineral
Sex	Creativity, Rejuvenation	Ecstasy	Genitals, Sacrum, Mouth, Throat	Fire
Power	Movement, Grounding, Doing	Intention, Will	Belly, Psoas, Adrenals, Limbs, Lumbar Spine	Earth
Emotional	Empathy, Intimacy	Love	Heart, Eyes, Hands, Skin, Thoracic Spine	Water
Thinking	Logistics, Belief	Classifying information	Left-brain	Air
Psychic	Wonder, Illumination	Intuition	Right-brain, Pineal gland	Electricity
Crown	Transcendence	Absorption in the Eternal	Upper skull, Pituitary, Corona radiata	Space

38

The Disharmony
Of Pairs Of Centers

Center Dominating	Center Dominated	Result
Sex	Root	Fetishism, Craving for pleasure
Sex	Power	Sadism, Masochism
Sex	Emotional	Romanticism
Sex	Thinking	Pornography
Sex	Psychic	Erotic or Romantic fantasizing
Sex	Crown	Devotionalism
Thinking	Root	Paranoia, Blind insecurity
Thinking	Sex	Promiscuity, Celibacy, Masturbation
Thinking	Power	Violence, Inertia, Politics
Thinking	Emotional	Sentimentality, Cynicism, Neediness
Thinking	Psychic	Fascination, Irony
Thinking	Crown	Idealism, Metaphysics
Root	Sex	Conventional marriage, Jealousy
Root	Power	Possessiveness, Cowardice
Root	Emotional	Misguided loyalty, Hysteria
Root	Thinking	Taboos, Belief systems, Impermeable logic
Root	Psychic	Occultism, Gullibility, Escapism
Root	Crown	Fundamentalism, God reduced to parent
Power	Root	Obsessive materialism, Defensiveness
Power	Sex	Rape
Power	Emotional	Preaching, Lack of empathy
Power	Thinking	Righteousness
Power	Psychic	Megalomania, New Age channeling
Power	Crown	Spiritual materialism, Egocentricity

Emotional	Root	Fanaticism, Patriotism
Emotional	Sex	False intimacy
Emotional	Power	Boasting, Do-gooderism, Martyrdom
Emotional	Thinking	Enthusiasm, Proselytizing, Melodrama
Emotional	Psychic	Hope, Nostalgia
Emotional	Crown	Religion
Psychic	Root	Superstition
Psychic	Sex	Voyeurism
Psychic	Power	Capitalism, Communism
Psychic	Emotional	Blind faith
Psychic	Thinking	Daydreaming, Impracticality, Confusion
Psychic	Crown	Dissociative mysticism, Theosophism
Crown	Root	Bureaucracy
Crown	Sex	Neurotic sublimation, Fake surrender
Crown	Power	Empire-building, Spiritual ambition
Crown	Emotional	Strategic Indifference, Career as a saint
Crown	Thinking	Poor discrimination, Cultic glibness
Crown	Psychic	Obsessive futurizing

39

What To Remember
When You Are In Emotional Pain

Jealousy, hatred, fear, greed, rage, sorrow — do not make a problem out of these, or you will simply be impaling yourself on your mind's "solutions," thereby only compounding your suffering, unnecessarily complicating it with abstraction, looking for answers in the artificial light of thought, desperately trying to *think* your way out of your apparent difficulty, not seeing that doing so only reinforces your entrapment...

Suppression of contracted emotional states only tightens their knot, exaggerating and, more often than not, relocating their point or area of eruption. Merely witnessing them usually is but a sophisticated escape from their intensity or rawness of feeling. Acting them out does not uproot them, but only strengthens their script. Remedial techniques, therapeutic and otherwise, only further mechanize us, doing little more than hobbling the sheer power of such feeling with dogma, guilt, rationalization, shoulds, prepackaged analyses, and articulately consoling excuses; in fact, the whole effort to "fix" emotional pain presupposes that such hurt is a disease, something to eradicate or domesticate, when it actually is something to face, penetrate, illuminate, and lovingly integrate, without robbing it of any of its untamed force and depth.

So what can be done? Confess your emotional pain, and confess it with unrehearsed vulnerability, empathetic sensitivity, and open-faced passion. Confess it with such vitality and heartbreaking honesty that your *primary* impulse is clearly and eloquently revealed, free of all merely mental representation. Let humour, not escapist, flip humour, but deep, ruthlessly accurate humour permeate, brighten, and amplify your confession, especially at its most dramatic or self-conscious.

Make exposure more important than composure. Reveal and give up your position. Give up being right. Give up being wrong. Give up your hidden grip. Lose face. Make space for a truer face.

Be specific as you're wild. Reclaim your roots and your wings. Don't play cool. Make room for your fool. If there is a surrounding sense of danger, real or not, use it to sensitize yourself, rather than to shrink or inflate yourself. Let your guilt thaw into shame, and let your shame flood you through and past all blame, until you settle into warmly expansive ease, *naturally* embodying responsibility instead of blame, without any diminishment of your passion.

The secret to working effectively with contracted emotional states is to enjoy your confession of them — this is not as difficult as it might sound, nor is it contrived. The point is not to smile away your pain, nor is it to cover up or deny the depths of what you are feeling; the point is deliberate expansion in the midst of contraction, not a peripheral or compensatory expansion (as in the fucking away of rage, or in the relief provided by sedation), but a *core* expansion, in which the energy of your emotional condition radiates out and out, without *any* overseeing of mind. Such opening, such intentional flowering, however outrageous its petals, is not only an act of great courage, but also an act that through its very animation is *self-illuminating*. It is a simple yet lucid exposure of our state, rather than a submission to its intentions; it is a vulnerable sharing, rather than just a mechanical spilling out of endarkened feeling and twisted need.

A full-bodied, heartfelt confession of jealousy, for example, can warm and cleanse all involved, deepening rather than obstructing intimacy — the sharp sense of separation and rejection felt in jealousy gradually dissolves in the generous heat of such confession, *naturally* transmuting into excitement, grief, connectedness, love, and free energy...

Insight will ordinarily be of little or no use prior to your confession, for it will all too likely be distorted by the viewpoint that characterizes your contracted condition. However, once your confession is underway and bright with its own momentum, truly valuable insight will often spontaneously arise, in multi-levelled harmony with your expansion. Do not try to force or create such insight; simply make room for it.

Jealousy, hatred, fear, greed, rage, sorrow — do not suppress these, do not rise above them, do not submit to their point of view, do not shrink from them, do not indulge them, do not try to think your way through them, do not try to meditate them into oblivion — *feel* them without *reacting* to them. Confess them. Reclaim the purity of feeling that lies twisted in their mind-polluted grasp. Go to the very heart of them; give them room to breathe, give them sky, give them permission to nakedly roar, cry, shout, whisper, and fly. Don't turn from their passion — *trust* it, *use* it, share it, unsnare it, letting its fire clear and lighten your way!

Without waiting any longer, however *right* you may *think* you are, unwrap the gift of your emotional pain, however dark it might be, and confess its contents with your all, letting your outpourings waterfall and stream through your heartland, trusting even the roughest currents of your breakout...

40

Awakening
Creates Its Own Morality

Those who lose touch with their fundamental nature find themselves subject to all sorts of moral codes — structures and ideologies ostensibly designed to better their condition are mechanically granted the right to invade, occupy, and represent them, whether in democratic, autocratic, or prophylactic terms. Attention is reduced to little more than an unilluminated focussing and fixation on the beliefs central to whatever moral code one has been most thoroughly propagandized into taking seriously. The price is integrity, the reward evasion of responsibility. In the realms of push-button morality, the converted tightly grip their personalized remote control, abandoning heart and soul for fast-food convenience for their snore. With a frighteningly intense automaticity, the illusion of immunity is packaged more and more skilfully, efficiently exploiting the marriage of belief and runaway consumerism, riding like a leech on the underbelly of every successfully marketed moral prescription. And, of course, the whole matter must be sanctified by Divine reference and approval — God is presented as either the Ultimate Parent, or as an ineffable Ideal, with pious hordes of egocentric go-betweens parroting guilt-reinforcing doctrines asparkle with supposedly divine shoulds...

Moral codes are but confessions of being estranged from Truth, because the stage upon which they are enacted is not naked, self-radiant Reality Itself, but only the terrain of sleeping minds, wherein ambitious dreamers concoct humanitarian schemes that have more to do with egoic manipulation than with real compassion. Moral codes are basically static; they imitate the Eternal in that they appear constant against a fluxing background. However, they are but empty shells, concretized swirls and twists of ingrown mind, desensitized, inhuman, and humorless, with the texture and reproducibility of the merely factual — they are bereft of magic and adaptive grace, being far too obsessed with the informational to be even close to the transformational.

Truth cannot be pressed and mounted, and presented to tomorrow, for it is forever fresh and vital, multidimensionally alive, not reducible to any blueprint, however metaphysically appealing — its very appearance and expression is in exact and graceful correspondence to its *current* circumstance. Truth does not make speeches, but is the very heartbeat of awakened speech, the spontaneous voicing and gesture of the lover, the one who does not make a monument out of his or her blossoming, but who only lives it with no compromise of bloom, freely emanating the fragrance of unpolluted Being, upending every alibi and honouring every goodbye and letting every kind of wind weave through his or her sigh...

Awakening creates its own morality. Its deepening requires a surrender not to rules, but to conducive conditions, conditions that contain within themselves (through the ongoing alertness of the participant) a capacity to hold form only as long as *necessary;* such conditions are not traps, or security-nets, but rather cocoons. If they are clung to or believed in, then they atrophy into caricatures of themselves, or rules.

Rules simply betray and obscure the awakening process, creating unnecessary associations between automatic obedience and various rewards, thereby chaining their devotees to hope and compulsive goal-orientation. No rules means anarchy and chaos only for childish and adolescent individuals — for those with a stably established center of being, no rules means permission to discover, structure, and yield to conditions supportive of further awakening. This is not conventional obedience, but rather conscious surrender. The alignment generated by rules is at best only a sophisticated parody of real harmony. To be in harmony does not mean that upheaval and upset don't occur, but that their very occurrence is used, fully used, as a gift of purification that leaves one in a deeper harmony with the dictates of one's core of being.

Implicit in this is trust, open-eyed trust. Such trust cannot be forced, but only embodied. It springs forth from an ethic beyond all mind-made moralities. Of course, there is a very real danger here, that catalyzed by those who claim to be the mediums or channels for such an ethic, and there is also an equally real danger of dismissing all such persons as charlatans, fools, or egomaniacs. Many are; perhaps almost all are. Yet some are not. But how can we tell? Liberate your intuition; learn to recognize the true from the false in yourself; find out where you are cultically inclined; cut through your craving to be perfectly parented. Fall in love with God, not with your favourite idea of God, not with your favourite personification of God, but with the Reality that is the Source and Substance of everything, the Infinite Mystery that now, at this very moment, is literally breathing you. If you must rise above your anger and hurt to feel this, then you are not feeling it, but are only setting up camp somewhere inside your skull.

God is not a vision, however sublime, nor an experience to be had in the crown chakra, nor a perfectly consoling Elsewhere, nor an infinite Should, nor the Overseer of any particular moral code. God is felt when the ordinary is embraced without any qualification whatsoever. God is felt when all belief is shed. God is felt when we stop making a problem out of Life. God is felt when spiritual ambition no longer attracts us. Without naked, unbound, unslumbering *feeling*, God is reduced to a goal, a remedy, a miracle cure, a sacred anaesthetic, a mere answerer to ego-centered prayers...

True trust obeys no moral code, however anarchistic. It is but the unexploitable, awakened faith of one who has left the promises of the mind for the already-present glory of their heartland. It is a joy, a fertile brilliance, a holy renewal, a yes that has room for every no, a yes both paradoxical and devastatingly simple, a yes wherein the elements dance and die, a yes aflame with the transcendence of blame, a yes already alive in you...

41

We Are Not "In" A Body

We cannot go out of the body, because we are not "in" a body. There is no true or lasting escape from the body, but only avoidance, metaphysical delusion, and emotional cowardice, or, at best, sublime expansiveness, transcendence of perception, and direct recognition of the body as pure energy, multi-dimensionally continuous with the rest of Existence.

What *is* within is our structuring, our physical, mental, psychic, and emotional anatomy, travelled, usually unconsciously, by the mechanism we call attention. And just *who* does the travelling (which all too often is but a repetitious touring of the shallows)? No one in particular, including the self-conscious knot of entrapping assumptions that so insistently refers to itself as *us*. There is no discrete entity inside, no independent inner dweller, but only the mechanical *personification* of the movement of attention through the body and mind (or, more precisely, through the bodymind).

What we essentially are makes its appearance not *in* a body, but *as* a body, gross or subtle.

The sense of separation that characterizes a so-called out-of-body experience is simply that, a sense of separation, a feeling of distance triggered by the settling of attention in zones of the brain that are ordinarily activated during dreaming. Attention thus focussed, deliberately (as in deep meditation or lucid dreaming) or not, generates experiences that seemingly occur beyond or independent of the body, when in fact such experiences are actually taking place in subtle, or seemingly non-physical, regions of the bodymind, registering their presence through the very same mechanisms as "ordinary" experience.

The physical dimension of the body drops off at Death, and we ordinarily feel lighter for a while, existing as a more rarefied bodymind moving through a dream-like realm pulsating with the fleshed-out consequences of our life's unillumined habits and hungers, as well as with the possibility of a truer life. Sooner or later, those longings of ours that are less than our longing for full awakening inexorably draw us toward another round of waking-state physicality, exactly fulfilling the current blueprint encoded throughout "us" both by our needs, and by what we are *doing* with our needs.

What we usually take ourselves to be is but (as was stated above) identification with the movement of attention through the bodymind, especially in the terrain of persona. However, this doesn't mean that there is no self at all, as is presumed in certain spiritual systems. There *is* self, identical with Infinite Being, beyond all assumptions and experiences of emptiness or non-being, simultaneously eternal and mortal, ecstatically and painfully alive, exquisitely individuated. This is what "we" must realize, from toe to crown — this paradoxical fullness is what we must embody and live, letting everything we are, high and low, merge and emerge in sacred reunion...

We are exactly what we are looking for, exactly! Our problem is that we look everywhere except inside our looking. Rarely do we notice just who is doing the looking, and even more rarely do we actually surrender to the eternal knowingness built into the very substance of our body.

Call it God's Joke. The body is the punchline. What is uncorked by getting the joke is the heart of the matter. The key is to *feel* your body, not from a mentalized distance, nor from a supposedly "higher" consciousness, nor from a place of cramped emotion, but *directly*, without any mediation or buffering — don't perceive it from your "headquarters," nor from any other dissociative point of view, but from a place of no-distance. This, done deeply and uninhibitedly, is the very heart of primordial vitality, carrying within itself an undying luminosity... Feel God, not with a little amoebic extension of yourself, but with your *entire* being. The feeling of God *is* God. Such feeling is not a matter of being inside or outside your physicality, but rather is about letting your *whole* bodymind, in all its dimensions, resonate with and express God.

Your body asks only to be loved, lived, and illuminated. The free body is the All of Existence, in the sense that it is, at every level, consciously continuous with all that is — it is the prism of Pure Being.

Your body is *not* an obstruction to realizing God. What matters is what we do with our bodies; the shift asked of us is from *having* a body to *being* a body. Even when the body dissolves in ecstasy, it still exists, as God's Body, pregnant with form.

In permitting a fuller, saner embodiment of our fundamental nature, we live as the Joy of the Source Itself, regardless of our moods and circumstances, regardless of the dramatics of purification.

This essay has no end. Nor does the body.

42

The Lover As Teacher

The lover who teaches the art of becoming fully human deliberately creates in his beginning students a dependency on him, a profoundly consuming dependency that, once well-rooted, he begins to simultaneously frustrate and illuminate, so that a healthier, more natural dependency can be established, one that is based not in helplessness or neurotic submission, but in a spirit-bright, deeply empathetic marriage of strength and vulnerability.

He does not fulfil his students' dreams, but artfully unveils and unravels them, again and again exposing and undressing his students' cravings for better or more "spiritual" dreams.

He at first earns his students' trust, then is given full trust, all the while never accepting blind trust, however tempting it might be to do so, steadily demanding the open-faced, emotionally naked revelation of his students' mistrust, doubt, and resistance, while teaching them the art of not making a problem out of such seeming obstacles.

He teaches only what he intimately knows.

He does not allow his students to make real estate out of moments of spirit-awakening, but rather sensitively, humourously, and dynamically exposes their neurotic self-positioning, leaving them not merely uprooted, but more and more receptive to recognizing and standing their true ground.

He is a safe place to let go of being safe.

He neither exploits nor denies the distance between him and his students, but only honours it by filling it to overflowing with his integrity, love, and wildness, directly and deeply meeting those of his students who move toward him with pure intent.

He opposes all cultism, including that which repeatedly forms around him, even if it means that all of his students must leave him.

He stays wounded, luminously wounded, avoiding the lure of indifference, detachment, and guru-positioning, thus remaining intimately associated with his students, clearly demonstrating that awareness and feeling need not be separated.

He offers only usable knowledge, teaching only according to the level of each student, teaching without prepackaging or rehearsal, spontaneously creating in each moment the most appropriate form for what he is transmitting.

He has no morality except that created by the awakening process.

He does not make an enemy out of his students' resistance, but welcomes it, using its force and shapings to instruct, without necessarily saying that he is doing so.

He is not a front for a system or doctrine, but rather a creator, an artist, an improvisational alchemist, whose designs and assignments fit the current needs of his students.

He is a passionately involved witness, a soulstirrer both rough and tender, a breaker and a mender, an excruciatingly lucid troublemaker, an exquisitely subtle and gutsy guide whose teaching occurs not as a career-urge, but because it is his very nature.

He *is* his teaching; if he isn't, he is only a preacher.

He, in everything he does, transmits his knowingness, so that his students absorb not only necessary knowledge, but, more importantly, the energy of his knowingness, the force and feel of it, in a manner that deepens their capacity for establishing true center in themselves, rather than in a manner that addicts them to his presence.

He asks for nakedness, giving not clothes, but climate.

His will must initially dominate that of beginning students, not only so strongly that apparent autonomy is yielded, but also in such a way that a deeper, more natural autonomy can emerge, an autonomy that is not neurotically independent, but that is the bright-bodied expression of being able to stand one's true ground without having to deify or institutionalize independence.

He is a doorway only the truly hungry can see, a doorway through which only the prepared can pass.

He uses everything as his classroom, including his mistakes.

He consistently weeds out true believers, converts, and fans.

He, knowing that beginners are all but incapable of real choice, takes away their so-called freedom of choice for a time, so that they can develop the capacity to make real choices.

He again and again freshly and artfully creates conditions that simultaneously challenge and nourish his students, teaching them how to enjoy living at their edge, showing them that to lose balance only provides an opportunity for a deeper balancing, as well as a truer parenting of oneself.

He creates rituals when necessary, but does not depend upon them.

He creates sanctuary for the awakening of the full human, simultaneously protecting and uncovering those who are with him, gradually revealing to them not only the art of welcoming the preparatory fire, but also the multi-dimensional significance of their awakening.

He is as vulnerable as he is powerful.

He does not so much shape students to his vision, as he lets his vision be shaped by his encounters with them.

He has no devotees, but only children, enemies, and allies.

He is a fire, a storm, a still lake, a whirlwind, a caress, a shove, a master of unveiling the obvious, a multi-armed midwife, a wise child, a deliberate sacrifice, a meeting-place of grief, laughter, and joy, a throbbingly human intersection of the everyday and the Everlasting.

He is an invitation that will not go away, an offer to come look and leap at the same time, a call to come make room for it all, now...

ROBERT AUGUSTUS MASTERS is a psychospiritual trailblazer and shamanic visionary, as well as a master therapist and teacher, an adept at getting to the heart of the matter, teaching only what he *intimately* knows, artfully, unswervingly, and potently serving as a multidimensional catalyst and medium for the awakening and embodiment of the full human. He is the guide of Xanthyros, a community both young and very ancient, in which awakening is the priority, not a dry, detached, or desireless awakening, but rather a vibrant, full-bodied, exquisitely practical awakening...

In Xanthyros, the difficult is not risen above, nor otherwise avoided, but is deliberately entered into *and* passed through with open eyes, until its energies, however dark or reactive, are *fully* and luminously integrated with the rest of one's being — this passage is simultaneously a solitary and communal effort, the structuring of which is neither prepackaged nor rehearsable, but is instead formed in earthy yet fluid correspondence with the *essential* imperatives of the *present* moment. This journey, which is not so much from here to there, as it is from here to a *deeper* here, honours no morality except that generated by awakening's alchemy. As such, Xanthyros serves the *real* needs of its members, rather than merely fitting them into an already designed system.

Xanthyros is an ever-evolving sanctuary for those whose longing to be truly free is stronger than their longing to distract themselves from their suffering. Xanthyros is also a fertile experiment, a passionate risk, a stand and a leap, an invitation and a sacred demand, a frameless doorway, a dynamic yet sweetly subtle crucible wherein the fire of the awakening process can do its work, not just in the transformative and revelatory meetings of Xanthyros, but also in its businesses, its children's school, and its ever-deepening transfamily intimacy...

A Novel Lucidly Intimate
With Awakening's Alchemy

LOVE
MUST ALSO WEEP

by
Robert Augustus Masters

LOVE MUST ALSO WEEP is both novel and catalyst; in its lucid sensuality, epiphanous breakthroughs, full-bodied emotion, exultant leaps, and dynamic yet subtly textured drama, it is highly entertaining reading, but it is also demanding, in that it engages far more than just imagination, artfully transporting the attentive reader not into the consoling terrain of fantasy (however seemingly "spiritual"), but right into the heartland of the Real. However, LOVE MUST ALSO WEEP is not mere exhortation, nor is it some kind of remedy or cure-all in novelistic form — it is a *direct*, multidimensional, vibrantly alive, exquisitely articulated honouring and expression of the Invitation to fully awaken, the Invitation That will not go away, the Invitation That is present in seed-form in *every* moment, asking only for our undivided attention. LOVE MUST ALSO WEEP is not about positive thinking, hope, nor any other compensatory strategy, but rather is about authentically facing what must be faced if we are to *truly* awaken from all the entrapping dreams we habitually animate, including our craving to dwell in a "better" dream.

LOVE MUST ALSO WEEP is at home with both suffering and ecstasy; it plunges with open eyes into the very core of Life, again and again finding expression at a level deeper than thought or belief, a level aglow with both natural integrity and self-illuminating passion. Its protagonist, Glam, is a spiritual adventurer, a warrior inside and out, a man simultaneously strong and vulnerable, already firmly and fluidly rooted in his being, yet ever allowing his deepest inner imperatives, however terrifying or bewildering, to direct his course. Gradually, he learns, and learns with his *entire* being, that nothing need be turned away from so that he might fully awaken — it all, however dense, violent, lustful, or endarkened, must be uninhibitedly faced, embraced, and passed through, not to be somehow left behind, but rather to be *included*, such inclusion being not a matter of naive acceptance, but of energetic transformation of such potency that even the most contracted or gross of conditions becomes but *available* Life-energy...

LOVE MUST ALSO WEEP does not sidestep or trivialize Paradox, nor replace it with metaphysical lullabies, but goes straight into It, seeking not meaning, but radical and unqualified revelation, until the very act of seeking lies in fertile ruins all around the naked Presence of living Truth. Glam's passage into and through so-called Darkness is one of both terror and rapture, aflame with labryinthine surprise and primal recognition. He doesn't overcome Darkness, nor does he rise above It, nor does he settle for trying to think, affirm, believe, or meditate It away — instead, he *literally* and luminously embodies It, both befriending It and freeing up Its energies for life-giving purposes. Put another way, he persists, until the Dark's in love with the Light, until Paradox is but Truth, until the Fire is but Light, until there is room for all in his being...

Glam's journey is none other than ours, our deepest journey, our truest trek, our jump from egocentricity to essence-centricity, our welcoming of the preparatory fire, our embracing of our heart's most sacred desire. However solidly framed LOVE MUST ALSO WEEP might appear, it is but a doorway to the Real, a highly dramatized yet just as highly transparent invitation to cut through all fantasy, so that every moment becomes Awakening's Moment...

Spontaneous Talks
by
Robert

Dolby B Chrome Cassette Tapes

MAKING GOOD USE OF TURNING POINTS

Turning points are times of extra energy, times of fertile chaos and potential transition; when we try to *think* our way through a turning point, we only confine its turbulent force in our minds, thereby intensifying our confusion, instead of letting its energies *fuel* our leap into a more fitting level of being. This talk, given October 27, 1988, is about how we must *consciously* blend with the currents of our turning points — we won't necessarily know where we are being taken, but we will not need to know, for we will inevitably be carried to a truer shore. Turning points need not be turned into crises; they are *not problems*, but wonderfully visceral confessions of our ripeness for a certain jump, or shift...

RELEASING SEX FROM THE OBLIGATION TO MAKE US FEEL BETTER

This talk, given October 7, 1988, is about freeing sex from its all-too-common chore of consoling us, whether through stress-discharge, pleasurable distraction, neurotic sublimation, or romantic delusion. If we pay *conscious* attention to ourselves in the midst of sex, we will see the underpinnings of our suffering with remarkable clarity — we will literally catch ourselves in the *act*, recognizing that what we tend to do sexually is but an exaggeration of what we do (or intend) when we *aren't* being sexual. When we stop depending on sex to make us feel better, we stop making a problem out of dependency itself, finding in ourselves a strength that is utterly *unthreatened* by dependency or attachment. Come toward sex *already* unstressed, *already* established in joy, letting it be a celebration of ecstatic intimacy, unburdened by any goal whatsoever...

THE ANATOMY OF EGO & SELF-ENTRAPMENT

Ordinarily, we exist as a self-enclosed, uneasily governed crowd of fragments, each one of which, when given sufficient attention, tends to refer to itself as "I" — however, all of these "I's" are not really selves, but are only *personified habits*. This talk, given October 23, 1988, is about shifting from ego-centricity (or unconscious identification with our dominant fragment of self) to essence-centricity, the point being not to annihilate ego, but to illuminate and purify it. All too easily, we seek release *not* from our self-entrapment, but from the pain of being *in* the trap, not truly realizing that the trap-door is *already* open, awaiting our passage, asking only that we let go of the *security* provided by our self-entrapment...

INTO THE HEART OF ENDARKENED MOODS

Instead of trying to escape or distract ourselves from our endarkened moods (which only reinforces their *roots*), we need to consciously confess *their* point of view and intentions, doing whatever we can to illuminate their terrain. In this talk, given November 22, 1988, the emphasis is on clearly exposing what we are *actually* doing while in unpleasant circumstances (inner or outer). Real happiness is not in fleeing "bad" moods, but rather is in going right to the very heart of them. Pure witnessing is of some use, but all too easily creates an unnecessary withdrawal from passion — the key here is to blend witnessing with *direct*, empathetic participation in our *feeling* dimension, knowing that *everything* we are must be fully faced, embraced, and passed through...

HAPPINESS IS NOT IN HAVING, BUT IN BEING

Real happiness is not in having, but in *being*. The expectation that *having something* (a relationship, an object, a certain feeling, a spiritual breakthrough) will make us feel better only intensifies our suffering, by *addicting* us to that particular something. This talk, given December 12, 1988, is about the nature of having, the need to shift from having to being, and the sane use of possessiveness. If we insist on having something, then it *has* us; on the other hand, if we rest in and *as* our being, then we can both enjoy and *deeply* participate in having, without becoming addictive about it...
(Concludes with a poem)

EMBODYING THE PASSIONATE WITNESS

This talk, given December 7, 1988, is about carrying alertness into the labyrinths of self-contraction, without any recoil from passion, desire, attachment, intimacy, or any other facet of a fully human life. Trying to escape the pain of our self-entrapment only creates more pain and more craving for pleasurably sedating release. The alternative to this is not resignation, nor more sophisticated strategies of escape (including those of all too many "spiritual" paths), but is simply to make room for our pain, letting its energies come unclenched, until they are but *available* Life-Force — this is *not* a technique, nor a recipe, but an always-fresh *art*, the very essence of which is the spirit-bright embodiment of the passionate witness, the one for whom turning away is no longer an attractive option...

ECSTASY CANNOT BE PRODUCED

The assumption that ecstasy is elsewhere, at the end of a series of steps, or at the point of maximal sexual stimulation, is not true — ecstasy exists in the *heart* of each moment, in the very depths that we flee in our compulsive searching for pleasurable release. This talk, given October 7, 1988, explores both ecstasy *and* its surrogates, emphasizing our need to *literally embody* a life free of all escapism and compensatory activity. Ecstasy is *not* addictive; only when we've turned away from ecstasy do we become addictive, simply because we then create dependency-relationships with whatever promises to deliver us from our suffering. Ecstasy is not a reward, nor is it a product — it is but the open face of real happiness, the pure shout of the awakened heart...

(Concludes with three poems)

RESPONSIBILITY IS THE GROUND OF FREEDOM

This talk, given August 29, 1988, is about not permitting *circumstantial* happiness to obscure our addictions, including that of ego, and it is also about the relationship between freedom and responsibility. For *real* freedom to exist, we must be responsible for creating and maintaining the environment, both inner and outer, that best supports such freedom. Without true responsibility, freedom is but licence, just an exaggerated kind of permission; without freedom, responsibility is but joyless duty, a burdensome obligation, polluted by well-dressed *blame*. As we awaken, it becomes increasingly clear that for every increase in freedom, there must also be a corresponding increase of responsibility...

AWAKENING CREATES ITS OWN MORALITY

Prior to awakening, we are infested by moral codes dictated by authority other than that native to ourselves, literally enslaving ourselves to inner and outer shoulds, worldly or other-worldly. This talk, given September 9, 1988, concerns the art of opening ourselves to the morality generated by the awakening process. Instead of rigidly conforming to rules, we need to create conditions conducive to the stage of our awakening, *without* addicting ourselves to the replication of such conditions — our activities thus become not a means *toward* happiness, but rather an expression *of* happiness. Peace then is for us not a repression of violence and primal force, but rather a passionate, *full-bodied* yes that includes within itself *every* no...

REAL RISK-TAKING

In this talk, given November 2, 1988, risk-taking is thoroughly explored. If we aren't willing to risk everything, then we'll only lose everything of *real* value. Sane risk-taking is not a matter of egocentric daring, but rather a matter of luminous intelligence and heartfelt gutsiness; it is a willingness to come undone, to let our binding familiarities come unstrung, and it is also a way of *directly* acknowledging the inherent insecurity of Life. It is crucial to dive into open-eyed intimacy, to dive deep, to again and again stretch to make the leap, to develop and honour relationships wherein it is safe to let go of being safe. Without risk, there is no ecstasy, no fullness of being...

FROM GUILT TO SHAME TO FREEDOM

Guilt is *not* a feeling, but a suppression of feeling, a psychophysical knottedness, a heart-numbing splitting of self that allows us to *continue* doing what apparently makes us "feel" guilty — put another way, guilt means we don't have to grow. However, guilt is but frozen shame. This talk, given November 16, 1988, describes the movement from guilt to shame to freedom, and from blame (the morality of guilt) to responsibility (the morality of *healthy* shame). Shame, when skilfully worked with, catalyzes a deep inner cleansing, a lucid, *heartfelt* acknowledgement of what was done, a warmly streaming catharsis of one's entire system, bright with both self-forgiveness and a return to wholeness, free of guilt's stalemated world...

TRUTH CANNOT BE REHEARSED

When we are committed to being other than ourselves, we are but beggars for applause, inner or outer, capable only of *re-acting*; we are haunted by stage fright, especially that of performing what *cannot* be performed. This talk, given November 21, 1988, is about acting, truth-telling, and identity. As we cease pretending that we aren't pretending, we become less and less concerned about others' approval of us, and our freedom of choice becomes more than just the dictates of our conditioning. We learn the art of giving ourselves without giving ourselves away, gradually ceasing to animate our reactivity, shining through our every role, realizing that there are no Oscars for awakening...

Ordering Information

BOOKS: LOVE MUST ALSO WEEP $16.95

             THE WAY OF THE LOVER   14.95

             ROOM FOR ALL   7.95

AUDIOTAPES: (Dolby B Chrome Real-time tapes, each with two talks by Robert; average length 80 minutes)

AWAKENING CREATES ITS OWN MORALITY /
ECSTASY CANNOT BE PRODUCED

INTO THE HEART OF ENDARKENED MOODS /
EMBODYING THE PASSIONATE WITNESS

RELEASING SEX FROM THE OBLIGATION TO MAKE US
FEEL BETTER / FROM GUILT TO SHAME TO FREEDOM

HAPPINESS IS NOT IN HAVING, BUT IN BEING /
RESPONSIBILITY IS THE GROUND OF FREEDOM

TRUTH CANNOT BE REHEARSED /
THE ANATOMY OF EGO & SELF-ENTRAPMENT

MAKING GOOD USE OF TURNING POINTS /
REAL RISK-TAKING

(Each tape is $12.95; a set of all six is $69.95)

All prices are in Canadian dollars, and include postage.

Order from: **XANTHYROS FOUNDATION**
P.O. Box 91980
West Vancouver, B.C.
Canada   V7V 4S4